A Legacy of Shetland Lace

A Legacy of Shetland Lace

The Shetland Times Ltd.
Lerwick
2012

A Legacy of Shetland Lace

ISBN 978-1-904746-76-8

First published by The Shetland Times Ltd., Lerwick, 2012.

British Library Cataloguing-in-Publication Data
A catalogue record for this book is available from the British Library.

Printed and published by
The Shetland Times Ltd.,
Gremista, Lerwick,
Shetland ZE1 0PX.

Dedication

This book is a tribute to the lace knitters who produced such delicate, intricate work, and to those who have kept these traditions alive. It is also a tribute to those who use lace knitting skills to push boundaries, challenging themselves and others to aspire to the inventiveness of those who inspired them. We hope it inspires you too.

Contents

Patterns

Introduction

The native breed of Shetland sheep has long been recognised as having fleece of exceptional fineness and soft handle, so it is not surprising that women in Shetland from a long time past have been skilled spinners and knitters.

In Unst, the most northerly isle of the Shetland group, women developed the special skill of spinning gossamer fine yarn to knit complicated lace patterns, fashioning shawls, scarves, veils, baby christening gowns etc, producing their designs from a number of different lace "motifs" grouped to make pleasing and artistic designs. While some of the motifs were possibly copies from lace, many originated in Shetland and were named after everyday things to do with the croft and the sea which surrounded their creators. Through export, the motifs and patterns and garments using them became known as Shetland Lace.

Through the early 19th century, some of these garments were shown in exhibitions in London, and a visiting London businessman found a market for these garments, and this became a successful commercial venture, providing much needed extra income for the knitters. The 1861 Unst census records that there were over 150 shawl knitters and 92 wool spinners in Unst. This was from a female population, aged fourteen and up, of 1296 of whom 158 were widows. Several of the garments found their way into royal households, both UK and abroad.

This trade declined in the earlier part of the last century with the advent of spinning mills and, subsequently, knitting machines which produced a better commercial return, so traditional fine lace knitting skills declined and the number of fine lace knitters was reduced to only a few. Some of the original hand knitted motifs were converted for use in machine knitting and factory production and have become ubiquitous in international shops and catwalks.

One of the aims of the Shetland Guild of Spinners, Knitters, Weavers and Dyers, founded in 1988, is to preserve and further Shetland's traditional textile heritage: hence the purpose of this book. It contains patterns designed by various members of the Guild, using traditional methods of constructing a design. Our ancestors knitted mostly garments using complicated patterns, but the patterns here have designs planned for all levels of skills and experience. Some of the designs are strictly traditional, some modernised to suit present day fashions, but all are knitted as in the olden days, ie each knitter fashioning her design from a known wide range of "motifs" which were at one time passed down from mother to daughter.

The knitters of the past lacked many of today's advantages. They had small spinning wheels, some made from driftwood, no graph paper to record their designs, indifferent lighting, and had often to take up their knitting after a hard day's work on the croft or in the croft house. They produced some quite remarkable and beautiful garments. It would be a pity if their skills became a wonder of the past.

Abbreviations and explanations

Shetland Guild of Spinners, Knitter, Weavers and Dyers logo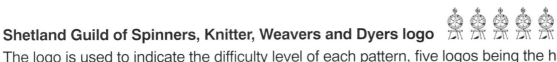
The logo is used to indicate the difficulty level of each pattern, five logos being the hardest.

Cast on

The cast on should be loose. Use your preferred cast on method, using a larger sized needle if necessary.

Cast off

Cast off should be loose, using a larger needle if necessary.

Tension

Our garments were measured after washing and dressing. You may wish to make a tension swatch of at least 40 stitches and 60 rows. For scarves, stoles and shawls tension is not crucial, but to ensure yarn requirements are adequate, tension should match that stated in patterns as near as possible.

Symbols used in charts

☐	Knit.
■	No Stitch.
⊟	Purl.
O	Yarn over.
O O	Yarn over twice. In the following row treat the 2 strands of yarn as separate stitches, and knit the first and purl the second.
＼	Slip 1, knit 1, pass slipped stitch over or knit 2 together through the back of the loop.
／	Knit 2 together.
⋏	Knit 3 together or slip 1, knit 2 together, pass slipped stitch over.
⩘	Increase by knitting into stitch twice.
V	With yarn at back, slip stitch onto right needle without knitting it.
●	Lock stitch. On a peaked edging, shows the stitch which the last cast off stitch has been passed over.
×	Cast off.
2	Work 2 together, either knit 2 together or slip 1, knit 1, pass slipped stitch over as instructed in individual pattern.
3	Work 3 together, either knit 3 together (2 stitches from edging and 1 stitch from main part) or slip 2, knit 1, pass slipped 2 over (2 stitches from edging and 1 from main part).
••	There are 2 stitches to be worked in this square.

Abbreviations used in written instructions

K	knit	P2tog	purl 2 together
P	purl	PM	place marker
yo	yarn over	RS	right side
K2tog	knit 2 together	WS	wrong side
K3tog	knit 3 together		

Shetland words associated with knitting

board	to put knitting on a wooden frame or a wooden frame used to dress/ stretch knitting
cole/coling	shape/shaping using decreases, eg for neckline
drappit/slippit loop	stitch accidentally slipped from needle
dressing	preparing the finished knitting to make it ready to wear
geng	one row regardless of whether it is knitted in the round or flat
hap	a shawl for everyday wear
hentilaggits/hentilaags	loose tufts of wool are often left on heather as sheep walk past or scratch themselves. These used to be collected for spinning.
hosiery	hand knitted garments
intaks	decreases
kemp	work hard to complete a piece of knitting, or to compete
lay on	cast on
lay up	start a garment
loop	stitch
love links	a vertical pattern of holes, worked every row, which separate quarters of a hap, or a lace edging from the main pattern of a stole or scarf
maakin/makkin	process of knitting, or a piece of knitting
maakin belt	knitting belt, made from leather and filled with horsehair
oo	sheep's wool
oppenwark	lace knitting
peerie	small
raas	rows
riggies	ridges in garter stitches
right loops	knit stitches
rooin	plucking wool off sheep – instead of clipping
sok	piece of knitting
scoor	to wash woollen garments
shawl	a shawl knitted in finer wool, and with more intricate patterns, than a hap
spret	when things go so wrong that you need to pull out the knitting needle and take back the last rows of knitting
steek/stik	another name for love links
sweerie geng	first row
tak dee sok	bring your knitting
wires	knitting needles
wirsit	wool spun into knitting yarn
wrang loops	purl stitches

Grafting

Grafting is a way of joining knitting pieces so that the join looks as if it is knitted, and is therefore almost invisible. Grafting can join a group of stitches to the side of a knitted piece, or join two knitted pieces.

Steaming stitches before grafting will help to stop them unravelling. You may find it easier to keep all stitches on knitting needles.

Stitches to be grafted need to be on two needles. It may be easier to put stitches on shorter knitting needles for grafting.

It is best to have the same number of stitches on both needles.

Make sure pieces to be grafted have wrong sides facing each other.

Use a blunt needle for grafting; the smallest size you can manage.

Grafting thread will go from right to left.

Stocking stitch graft

Place the needles holding the two sets of stitches together, with wrong sides in the middle. The needle with the long end of wool should be at the back, and the wool at the right hand end. Thread the wool in a tapestry needle.

Put tapestry needle in the first stitch on the front needle, as if to purl, draw wool through but do not slip the stitch off the needle. Pass tapestry needle under the front needle and put it in the first stitch on the back needle as if about to knit, draw wool through but do not slip the stitch off the needle. Bring tapestry needle again to front under the first needle.

Put tapestry needle in the first stitch on the front needle, as if to knit, draw wool through and slip the stitch off the needle; put tapestry needle in next stitch on front needle, as if about to purl, draw wool through but do not slip the stitch off the needle. Pass tapestry needle under the front needle and put it in the first stitch on the back needle as if about to purl, draw wool through and slip the stitch off the needle; put tapestry needle in next stitch on back needle, as if about to knit, draw wool through but do not slip the stitch off the needle. Bring tapestry needle again to front under the first needle.

Repeat from * to *

When you have one stitch on both needles, put the tapestry needle in the stitch on the front needle, as if to knit, draw wool through and slip the stitch off and lay front needle aside. Put the tapestry needle in the stitch on the back needle as if about to purl, draw wool through and slip the stitch off the needle. Fasten off.

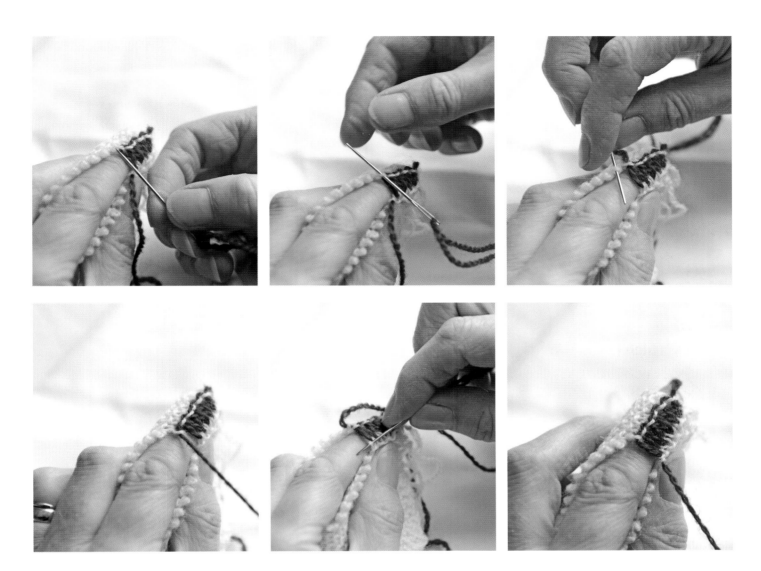

Garter stitch graft

Place both needles holding the two sets of stitches side by side, with the garter stitch ridge close up to the needles. Slide one needle behind the other; the needle with the long end of wool should be at the back, and the wool at the right hand end. The back needle should have the ridge next to the needle on the inside and the front needle should have the ridge next to the needle on the outside.

Thread the wool in a tapestry needle.

Put tapestry needle in the first stitch on the front needle, as if about to purl, draw wool through but do not slip the stitch off the needle. Pass tapestry needle under the front needle and put it in the first stitch on the back needle as if about to purl, draw wool through but do not slip the stitch off the needle. Bring tapestry needle again to front under the first needle.

* Put tapestry needle in the first stitch on the front needle, as if to knit, draw wool through and slip the stitch off the needle; put tapestry needle in next stitch on front needle, as if about to purl, draw wool through but do not slip the stitch off the needle. Pass tapestry needle under the front needle and put it in the first stitch on the back needle as if about to knit, draw wool through and slip the stitch off the needle; put tapestry needle in next stitch on back needle, as if about to purl, draw wool through but do not slip the stitch off the needle. Bring tapestry needle again to front under the first needle.*

Repeat from * to *.

When you have one stitch on the needles, put the tapestry needle in the stitch on the front needle, as if to knit, draw wool through and slip the stitch off and lay front needle aside. Put the tapestry needle in the stitch on the back needle as if about to purl, draw wool through and slip the stitch off the needle. Fasten off.

Moss stitch graft

Grafting moss stitch is tricky but there is just one pattern, Laureya, which needs moss stitch grafting over 13 stitches.

Place both needles holding the two sets of stitches side by side. Slide one needle behind the other; the needle with the long end of wool should be at the back, and the wool at the right hand end. Thread the wool in a tapestry needle.

Put tapestry needle in the first stitch on the front needle, as if about to purl, draw wool through but do not slip the stitch off the needle. Pass tapestry needle under the front needle and put it in the first stitch on the back needle as if about to purl, draw wool through but do not slip the stitch off the needle. Bring tapestry needle again to front under the first needle.

* Put tapestry needle in the first stitch on the front needle, as if to knit, draw wool through and slip the stitch off the needle; put tapestry needle in next stitch on front needle, as if about to knit, draw wool through but do not slip the stitch off the needle. Pass tapestry needle under the front needle and put it in the first stitch on the back needle as if about to knit, draw wool through and slip the stitch off the needle; put tapestry needle in next stitch on back needle, as if about to knit, draw wool through but do not slip the stitch off the needle. Bring tapestry needle again to front under the first needle. Put tapestry needle in the first stitch on the front needle, as if to purl, draw wool through and slip the stitch off the needle; put tapestry needle in next stitch on front needle, as if about to purl, draw wool through but do not slip the stitch off the needle. Pass tapestry needle under the front needle and put it in the first stitch on the back needle as if about to purl, draw wool through and slip the stitch off the needle; put tapestry needle in next stitch on back needle, as if about to purl, draw wool through but do not slip the stitch off the needle. Bring tapestry needle again to front under the first needle.*

Repeat from * to *.

When you have one stitch on the needles, put the tapestry needle in the stitch on the front needle, as if to purl, draw wool through and slip the stitch off and lay front needle aside. Put the tapestry needle in the stitch on the back needle as if about to purl, draw wool through and slip the stitch off the needle. Fasten off.

Voxter scarf before dressing. Red thread indicates right side.

Finishing

Dressing is the final step once the knitting has finished; it transforms the lace. Shetland wool has a 'memory' so will keep its shape once it has been stretched. Note: if you use wool which has been treated to be machine washable it is unlikely to hold its shape.

Opinions vary on how much to stretch. Some say the lace should be stretched as much as possible while others advise that it must not be overstretched.

Make sure all yarn ends are woven in, but not trimmed, before washing.

Lace knitting needs to be stretched while it is damp. Before you wash your finished piece, make sure you read all the instructions for dressing so that you have everything you need, and items are ready to be stretched as soon as they are washed. Temporarily joining scarves, stoles and open fronted garments into tubes makes dressing easier.

For this you will need a blunt tapestry needle and cotton thread in a contrasting colour.

If you want to dry the item on a flat surface, you need rustless pins. Stretching flat on squared cotton material is useful for getting everything straight.

For garments, a jumper board is the best but stretching flat, on squared cotton material, using rustless pins, blocking wires and dowling rods works well.

Preparation for dressing

It is important to follow these steps before you wet your knitted piece.

Scarves or stoles

Either put the short edges together, or put the long edges together, folding in the middle. Choice will depend on length and width and size of available board.

This gives an oblong, open on three sides. The long sides need to be joined to make a tube, open at one narrow end. Note: If you are drying on a flat surface, folding the scarf or stole means you need less space and fewer pins but there is no need to sew edges together.

If the scarf or stole has scalloped edges, join the peaks individually with cotton thread, making sure the ties are the same length, and loose enough for scissor points to get in to cut them away once the item is dry.

If the sides are straight, there is a choice of two methods

(a)   whip stitch the long loops between the ridges with a cotton thread.

(b)   baste the sides together with cotton thread, one stitch in from the edge.

If no suitable wooden frame is available, select a long narrow piece of strong cardboard – it should be approximately a sixth wider than the tube and a third longer.

Gently pull the dry scarf or stole over the cardboard, just to make sure it is neither too wide nor too narrow, and that the cardboard is long enough. (The scarf or stole will stretch quite a bit when damp.) Adjust the cardboard width till satisfied, but do not shorten the length.

Cover the cardboard with either clingfilm and/or parcel tape. This gives smooth edges.

Triangular shawl and hap

Count points of shawl to make sure you have enough rustless pins for each point.

Make sure you have a space where it will be undisturbed for a day. If available, use a stretcher for the hap.

Garments

Using cotton thread, whip stitch the long loops between the ridges on the fronts together – this will be removed later so don't secure the ends too well.

For Laureya, stop when you get to the start of V neck shaping.

For Laureya, start at V neck shaping on right front, put cotton thread, from back to front, through the long loops up the side, round the back neck and down the left front.

For Gairdins, using cotton yarn and tapestry needle, starting at right front edge, put thread, from back to front, through each neck stitch.

For necks of both Laureya and Gairdins, leave two long ends of cotton – these will be tied in a bow when dressing.

Decide how you are going to dress this top, and get everything ready.

Washing

Hand wash in warm, not hot, water using a product suitable for washing wool. Rinse at the same temperature.

Roll in a clean towel to remove excess moisture.

Dressing

Scarves or stoles

Gently pull the damp scarf or stole over the cardboard, making sure the sides are straight.

Gently stretch the scarf or stole lengthways.

If necessary, cut excess length from cardboard, covering cut edge with parcel tape.

Join the open end to match the other sides, thus securing the cardboard in the middle.

Leave till completely dry before carefully cutting the cotton threads, and trimming any ends.

Triangular stole and hap

Gently stretch the shawl, securing each point and ensuring that the edges are straight and equal in length.

Garments

Use jumper board if you have one or spread the garment on a flat surface and pin to shape using blocking wires, dowling rods and rustless pins.

Keep checking the shape.

Take care to check that sleeves both measure the same width and length.

Gently pull the neck thread to make a smaller size and tie in a bow.

Check that all the knitting is stretched and smooth. Adjust as necessary.

Everything

Leave till completely dry before carefully cutting the cotton threads, removing pins etc.

Trim all ends.

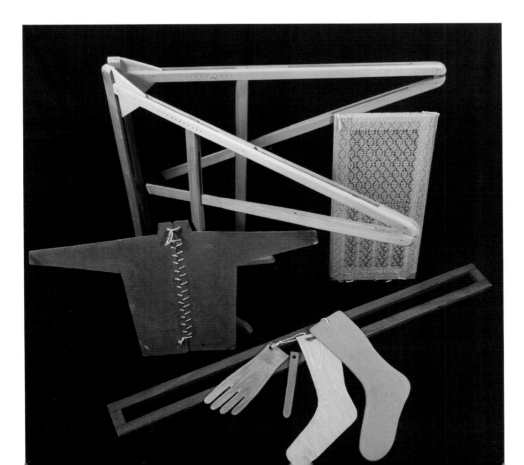

Suppliers

Shetland yarn used for designing the patterns in this book was either hand spun or bought from Jamieson's of Shetland, Jamieson & Smith or Shetland Organics. Where hand spun was used to design the pattern, the equivalent commercial wool was used for test knitting, and details are given for each pattern.

Jamieson's of Shetland (www.jamiesonsofshetland.co.uk)

Double Knitting:	25g; approx 75m
Shetland Heather:	50g; Aran weight; approx 92m
Spindrift:	2 ply; jumper weight yarn; 25g; approx 105m
Ultra:	2 ply; blended 50% Shetland wool/50% lambswool; 25g; approx 194m
Cobweb Ultra:	1 ply; blended 50% Shetland wool/50% lambswool; 25g; approx 390m

Jamieson & Smith (www.shetlandwoolbrokers.co.uk)

Soft Spun Chunky:	100g; approx 120m
2 ply jumper weight:	25g; approx 115m
2 ply lace weight:	25g; approx 169m
Supreme jumper weight:	50g; approx 172m
Supreme lace:	25g; 1 ply; approx 400m
Supreme lace:	25g; 2 ply; approx 200m
Cobweb:	25g; 1 ply; approx 350m

Shetland Organics (www.shetlandorganics.com)

Certified organic Shetland wool, Single ply:	25g
Certified organic Shetland wool, jumper weight:	50g; 2 ply
Certified organic Shetland wool, chunky:	50g; 3 ply

Retro-reflective yarn can be sourced from a variety of on-line traders

Vinstrik Scarf

Designed and knitted by Mary Kay. This scarf is a "straight through" design so no grafting is required. This scarf is named after the croft in Unst where Mary's grandmother grew up.

Materials:
2 x 25g balls Shetland Supreme 1ply lace yarn

2 x 2.75mm (UK 12, USA 1) knitting needles

Sizing:
Length 105 cm (41 in.) Width 25 cm (10 in.)

Tension:
33 stitches, 56 rows for 10 cm (4 in.)

Pattern Notes:
In chart B, rows 9 to 15 and rows 58 to 64 need extra concentration as the geometrical shape of the pattern is less obvious in these rows.

Instructions:
Cast on 79 stitches.
Knit 2 rows.

Start by knitting the 10 rows of chart A reading from the right hand side. All even rows read from left.
Knit 4 rows.

Now follow chart B for the 98 rows.
Knit this chart again 4 times, making a total of 5 complete patterns. Finish by knitting chart B again but finishing this time with row 74.
Knit 3 rows.

To complete the design, knit chart C.
Knit 2 rows and cast off loosely.

Follow washing and dressing instructions as given on page 15

"Stitch numbers were usually counted in scores.

Mary Kay

In common with all young Shetland girls of the time, Mary learned to knit as a young girl. She started by making jumpers for teddy bears. She learned without written instructions or patterns; by getting the number of loops from her mother, and then learned to work it out for herself.

By the time she was eleven years old she was knitting scarves, gloves and jumpers. The inhabitants of Cunningsburgh in Shetland are particularly well known for expertise in knitting gloves. At age twelve Mary spent a holiday there, learning to knit Fair Isle patterned gloves and generally improving her glove making skills. Shortly after she learned open work as well.

At that time there was a demand in the local hosiery shops for knitted garments so these were useful skills and brought welcome pocket money and income for schoolgirls, students and housewives. Mary sold some of her knitting to earn pocket money before leaving Shetland to study.

After some years Mary learned to spin, becoming quite addicted and for a while she cast her knitting aside! Having achieved the ability to spin fine lace yarns, she returned to knitting in order to use her hand spun wool. She has become thoroughly absorbed in designing and knitting lace, and likens lace knitting to drawing. She sells scarves through the Shetland Museum shop and occasionally designs scarves for Jamieson & Smith.

Mary has taught fine lace spinning for the National Spinning Guild. Most summers she delivers a workshop in lace knitting for visitors to Shetland. She has won many prizes both within and outwith Shetland for her knitting, and has demonstrated on many occasions, always encouraging others to try to learn too.

Vinstrik Scarf chart A

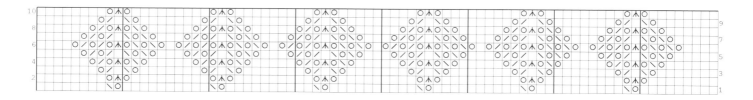

Vinstrik Scarf chart B

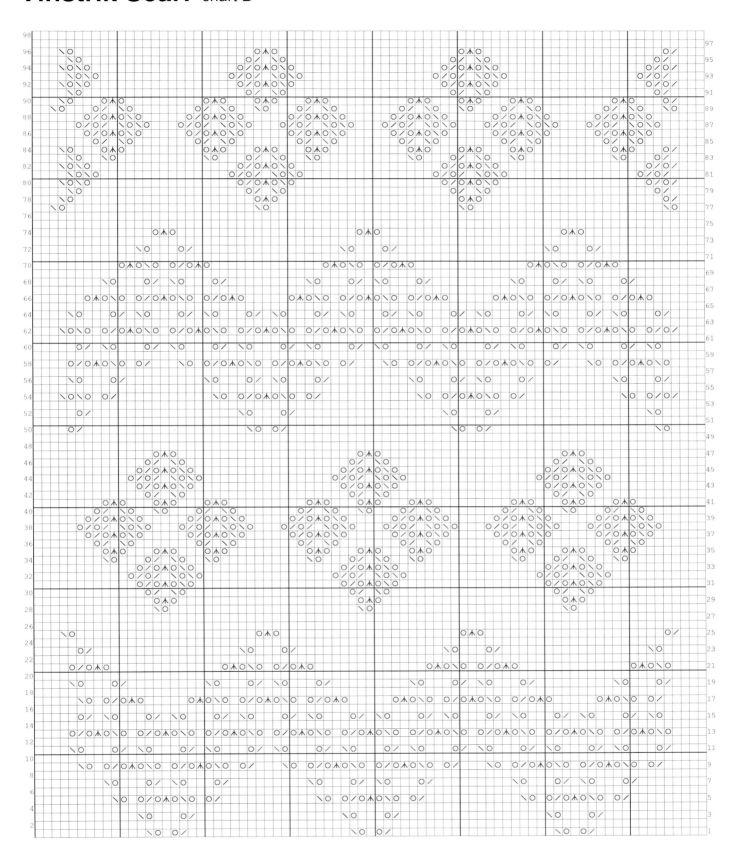

Vinstrik Scarf chart C

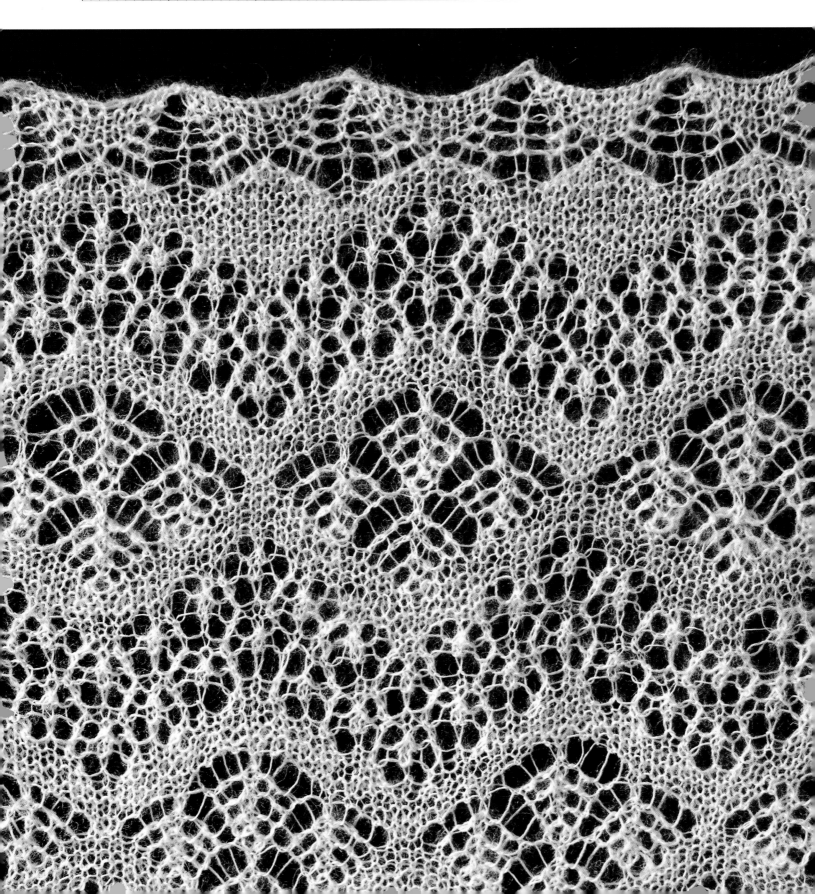

Cuckron Scarf

Designed by Sue Arthur This scarf was designed and knitted by Sue in Shetland hand-spun yarn equivalent in thickness to 1ply lace yarn. Sue named the Cuckron Scarf after her family's croft. Cuckron is the sound made by the burn (stream) as it runs past the house. This little, narrow scarf was designed for an elderly aunt who wanted a light scarf to keep the draughts off her neck.

Materials:
1 x 25g ball
100% Shetland 1 ply yarn

2 x 2 mm (UK 14, USA 00)
knitting needles

Sizing:
Length 91cm (36 in.)
Width 15 cm (6 in.)

Tension:
34 stitches, 72 rows
for 10 cm (4 in.)

Pattern Notes:
This scarf is knitted right through without the need to graft. The pattern is knitted every row and gives a very lacy effect. The motifs used are spider lace diamonds framed by 'steeks' or 'love links' on the long edges.

Instructions:
Very loosely cast on 49 stitches. Knit 4 rows
NB. Read chart from right starting at row 1 and from left on all even numbered rows.

Follow chart A from 1 to 61
Repeat rows 22 to 61 for as many times as required.
In this instance, 14 repeats were knitted.

Follow chart B to row 35
Work row 36 to complete design.
Knit 4 rows to finish scarf.
Cast off loosely.

Follow washing and dressing instructions as given on page 15

Sue Arthur

Sue was taught to knit by her mother and Grannie before she was ten years old.

She has always knitted for pleasure and to make clothes for the family and gifts for the family and close friends.

She particularly likes knitting all-over Fair Isle jumpers and any lace items.

While she was a member of The Coventry Guild of Weavers, Spinners and Dyers, she won the Guild of Broadweavers' trophy several times for handspun and knitted items.

In Shetland, she has won prizes for hand spun all-over Fair Isle garments and hand spun lace garments both in the Shetland Guild and at local Agricultural Shows. In 2011 she won the overall champion's trophy at the Voe Show for her fine hand spun hand knitted stole. One of Sue's Fair Isle jumpers is featured in "Real Shetland Yarns" which was published in 2012.

She has demonstrated both at Shetland Textile Working Museum and Shetland Museum as well as at various public events in Shetland. She tries to encourage people she meets on such occasions to try their hand at spinning and knitting. She has taught her daughter to spin and knit.

She hopes that this book will also encourage people to take up their knitting 'wires' and have a go.

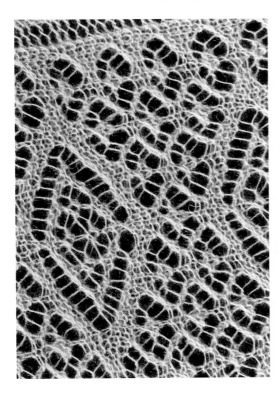

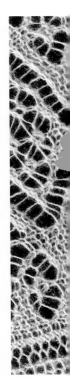

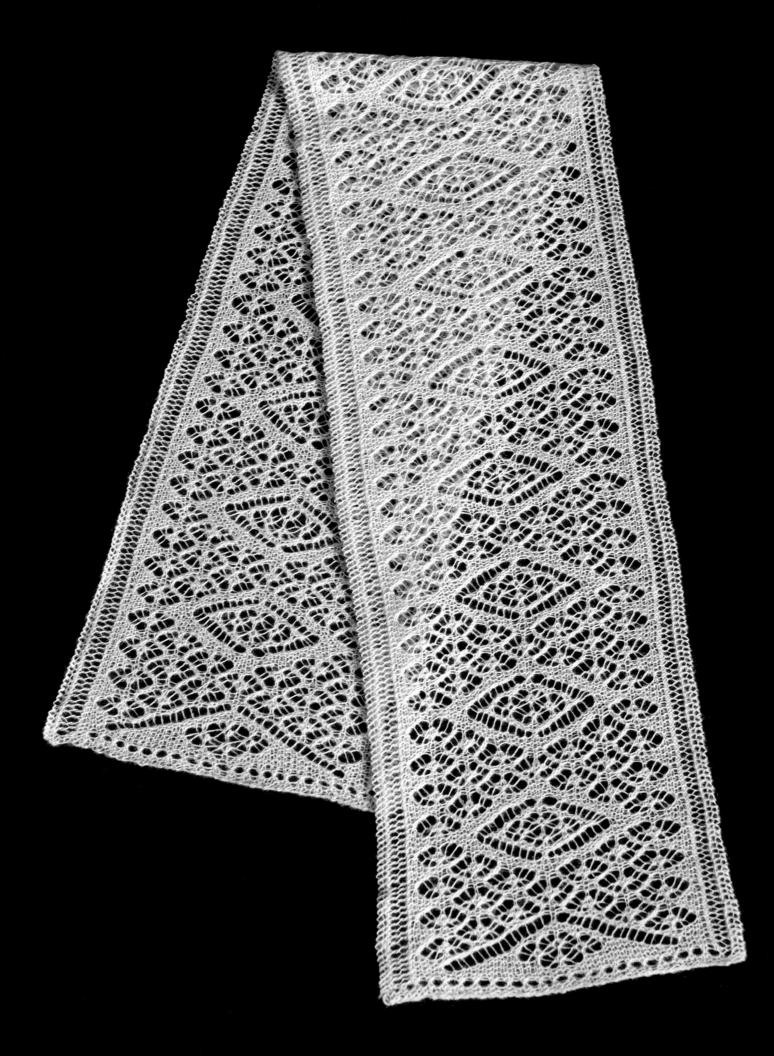

Cuckron Scarf chart A

Cuckron Scarf chart B

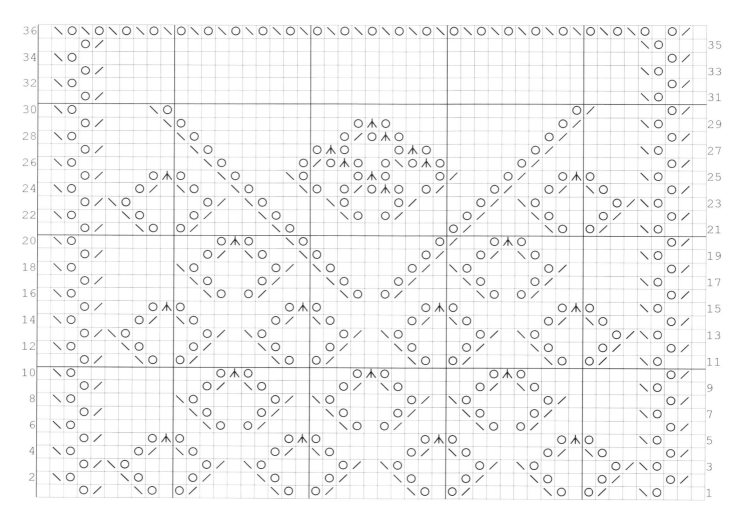

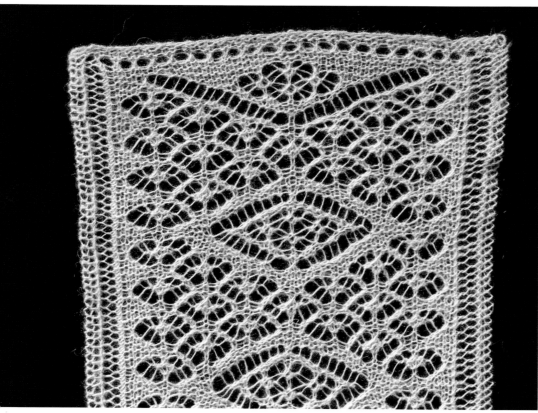

"Come laangerin some night" was an invitation to visit, and sharing knitting time would lift the boredom of knitting alone with no-one to speak to.

Reawick Scarf

Designed and knitted by Kathleen Anderson. This scarf shares its name with the village on Shetland's West Mainland where Kathleen has lived for many years.

Materials:
1 x 25g ball 100% Shetland 1 ply yarn

2 x 2 mm (UK 14, USA 00) knitting needles

Sizing:
Length 107 cm (42 in.)
Width 23 cm (9 in.)

Tension:
36 stitches, 64 rows for 10 cm (4 in.)

Pattern Notes:
This scarf is knitted in garter stitch with the pattern continuing throughout and does not require grafting. The pattern consists of 3 columns of cable pattern separated by the 'peerie bead' pattern which also outlines the two sides and ends of the design.

Instructions:
Cast on 81 stitches.
Knit 3 rows in garter stitch.

Start by following chart A reading pattern from the right.
Even number rows read from left.
The 8 rows of this pattern are knitted once to form the border.

Continue by following chart B starting at Row 1 on the right.
The 16 rows of this chart form the cable pattern.
Repeat this chart 44 times.

Complete the pattern of the scarf by knitting chart C rows 1 to 8.
Knit 3 rows in garter stitch.
Cast off.

The scarf should then be dressed using the method described on page 15

Kathleen Anderson

Kathleen learned to knit from her mother around age five. She sold her first items, child's Fair Isle mittens, aged about thirteen. Her mother 'finished' jumpers and cardigans for Tulloch's of Shetland and Kathleen's mittens were sold through them too.

Since then Kathleen has always earned some income from her knitting. At one time she 'finished' 20 jumpers a week and made a hand knit lace scarf at the weekend! For ten years she made machine knit plain jumpers.

Since 1990 she has concentrated on hand knitted Shetland lace. Kathleen says: "what I love knitting most are 1 ply lace shawls. I use many patterns. I would get bored doing the same patterns over and over again. I also change patterns to suit the number of stitches."

She has won many prizes and trophies for her knitting both in Shetland and at the Royal Highland Show in Edinburgh. As well as selling lace knit scarves through the Shetland Museum shop, her scarves and shawls are sold privately. These are internationally sought after, her last piece going to a buyer in Japan. She was commissioned to make a scarf for the late Queen Mother's 100th birthday.

Kathleen has demonstrated at the National Museum of Scotland as well as various venues in Shetland and Ireland. She is keen to pass on her knowledge and skill and to this end she teaches an evening class in Shetland lace during the winter.

She hopes this book will inspire and encourage young folk to take up Shetland lace knitting.

Raewick Scarf chart A

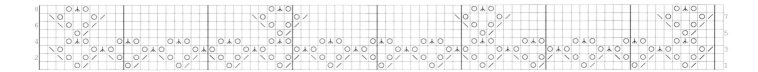

Raewick Scarf chart B

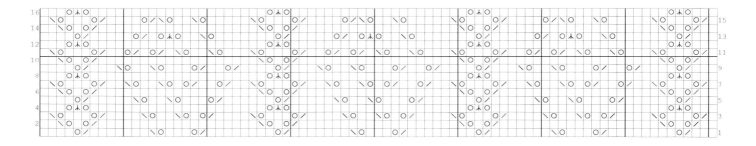

Raewick Scarf chart C

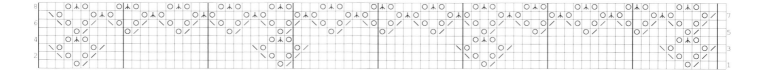

Smooth fingers are essential for fine lace knitting! In the past buttermilk was used to soften skin before starting to knit.

Hesta Scarf

Designed and knitted by Hazel Tindall. This scarf is knitted in a thicker yarn with patterns in each end and a pattern of holes forming a definition round the edge. This scarf is named after the croft, Hestataing, where Hazel grew up.

Materials:
2 x 50g balls Soft Spun
100% Shetland Chunky wool

2 x 4mm knitting needles (UK 8, USA 5)

Sizing:
Length 97 cm (38 in.)
Width of centre 10 cm (4 in.)
Ends 18 cm (7 in.)

Tension:
21 stitches, 28 rows for 10 cm (4 in.)

Abbreviations:
skp = slip one stitch, knit one stitch, pass the slipped stitch over
2tog = knit two stitches together
K = knit
o = wool over or 'cast up'

Pattern Notes:
This pattern is knitted in garter stitch throughout and no grafting is required. The scarf has slots on one end to allow the other end to be pulled through, thus making a cross-over neck tie style.

Instructions:
Cast on 3 stitches. All even rows knit.

Reading pattern from the right, start on chart A and complete to row 52. (21 stitches)

It is time to start making the slots for the scarf end.

Insert a marker in the edge stitch.

Work on the first 7 stitches. Keep pattern at outside edge following the chart of K1 o skp K4.

Repeat until 38 rows (19 holes) knitted. Break yarn leaving 20 cm tail

Now work on centre 7 stitches only, knitting every row for 40 rows, (20 ridges). The extra rows allow the scarf to lie flat. Break yarn

Now rejoin yarn to inside edge of last 7 stitches. Keep pattern at outside edge: K4 2tog o k1.

Repeat till 38 rows (19 holes) knitted. Break yarn. Put all stitches on one needle. Re-start at outside edge of first strip.

Knit 142 rows over all 21 stitches keeping the single hole pattern correct along the edges.

Follow chart B to complete the scarf, finishing at row 45.

Cast off remaining 3 stitches.

Finish scarf carefully according to instructions on page 15.

Hazel Tindall

Hazel is not sure which female taught her to knit – her mother, grandmother, older sister and aunt all lived in the same house, and all were knitters. Most Shetland girls used to learn to knit before they went to school. Her earliest knitting memory is of studying her knitting, trying to distinguish between knit and purl stitches.

Hazel's first love is Fair Isle knitting, and she knitted her first all over Fair Isle cardigan for herself when she was eleven. Throughout her teenage years she knitted Fair Isle yokes for jumpers and cardigans for various local businesses; this gained valuable pocket money.

In her early teens, intrigued by lace knitting done by her older cousins, she was told it was too difficult – but she could carry on with Fair Isle! She was in her late twenties before she tried lace knitting and can well remember the magic of the scalloped edge of the cockle shell.

Nowadays she rarely sells knitting as few people are prepared to pay what she asks. She knits garments for herself and family, usually putting them to a local show before they get worn. She writes knitting patterns which takes much longer than knitting the originals. Patterns can be found on www.hazeltindall.com.

As well as demonstrating, she has led knitting and crochet classes in Shetland. Fair Isle and lace knitting has taken her to other parts of Britain as well as Canada and America (twice to Handweaver's Guild of America's Convergence and several times to John C Campbell Folk School in North Carolina). She won competitions for knitting at speed in 2004 and 2008.

Being a member of the Guild gives her the opportunity to meet, and learn from, other knitting enthusiasts. Helping prepare this book has rekindled her interest in knitting lace.

Hesta Scarf chart A

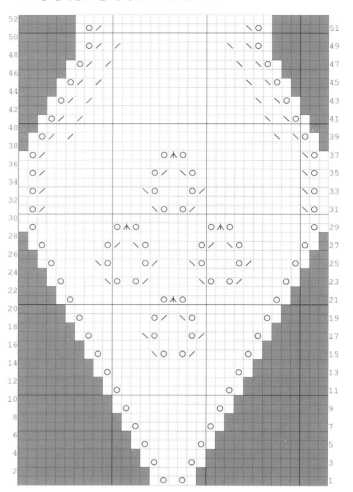

Hesta Scarf chart B

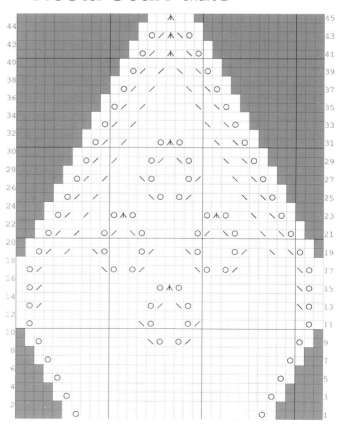

Vaga Scarf

Designed and knitted by Zena Thomson.
This scarf was designed and knitted by Zena using 1 ply Shetland Cobweb yarn and the name comes from the old name for her native Walls.

Materials:
1 x 25g ball 100% Shetland 1 ply yarn

2 x 3.25 mm (UK 10, USA 3) knitting needles
1 spare needle or stitch holder
Tapestry needle for grafting

Sizing:
Length 108 cm (46 in.)
Width 28 cm (11 in.)

Tension:
25 stitches, 27 rows for 10 cm (4 in.)

Pattern Notes:

This scarf is knitted in 2 parts. The horseshoe pattern repeats at both ends with the arrow pattern repeated through the middle. The end patterns and the middle are separated by knitting according to chart B as explained in instructions. Both parts are then grafted together.

"Wha haes a guid or an ill fit." It was always noted if a visitor came in when a new garment was just starting. If a visitor was already believed to have an 'ill fit', the knitting was likely to be re-started. If knitting went wrong after it was underway, the knitter would remember who had visited when it was newly started.

Zena Thomson

Zena started knitting on a cotton reel with four pins on top. She then moved to knitting with needles. This she learned from her mother and could knit in this way before she started school.

She started selling things she had made in a local shop in Walls when she was ten years old, the first thing being a pair of mittens. She also knitted vests, socks and other garments for her brothers and sisters. Zena was often asked to stay behind at school, not as a punishment but in order to help her teacher with her knitting!

In time she became a knitting instructor and worked for 20 years in the local schools. She now hosts a weekly knitting group in her own home during the winter. She is also keen to help other guild members when asked, and enjoys the added interest of encountering an unusual pattern or design.

Selling her hand knitting has helped family finances in years gone by. She still sells her knitting through the local shop, the Shetland Museum shop, and very often gets commissions from old friends throughout the world.

Zena has won many prizes from shows in Shetland and at the Royal Highland Show in Edinburgh for both Fair Isle and lace. Exhibiting at the Royal Highland Show led to Zena being commissioned by Buckingham Palace to design and knit a Shetland lace shawl for the Queen to present to the Empress of Japan on her visit to the UK in 1998. The Queen requested the cockleshell pattern and Zena incorporated this into the shawl.

Zena hopes the clear patterns and photographs in this book will help people to try out patterns they might otherwise not have tried. She would like if it helped to keep traditional knitting and lace patterns alive.

Instructions:

* Cast on 71 stitches and knit 1 row.

Follow chart A for horse-shoe pattern (10 rows).

Row 1 start reading pattern from the right.

Row 2 and all even rows start reading from left. Note that the edge detail of 'love links' pattern continues on every row.

Repeat these rows another 8 times making 9 completed horse-shoe strips.

Leave this piece of knitting on a spare needle or stitch holder.* Break yarn.

Repeat from *to*.

Now knit chart B (6 rows) and when this has been completed, move on to chart C, the Arrow pattern. Repeats of this pattern make the middle part of the scarf. Work the 12 rows of this pattern (chart C) 19 times altogether (more or fewer repeats for a longer or shorter scarf).

Finish by knitting the first 2 rows of pattern C.

Knit the first 5 rows of chart B.

Graft the two pieces together using garter stitch grafting as described in notes on page 12.

Wash the scarf carefully and dress according to instructions on page 15.

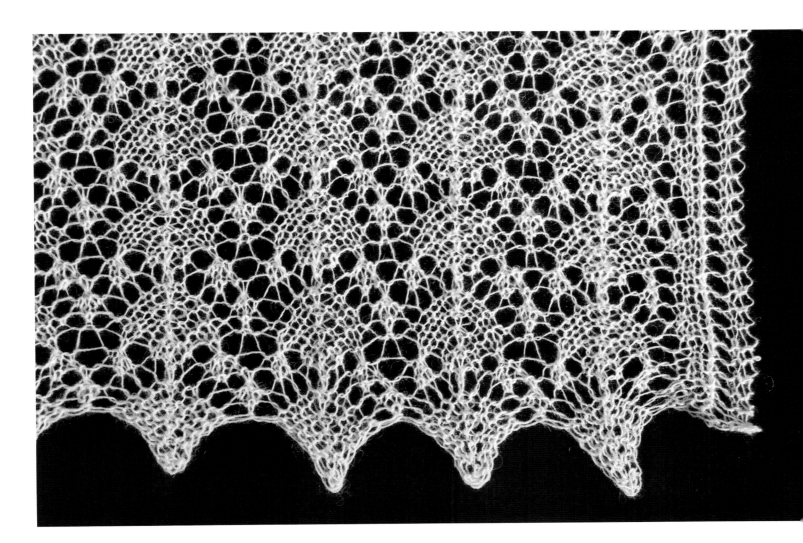

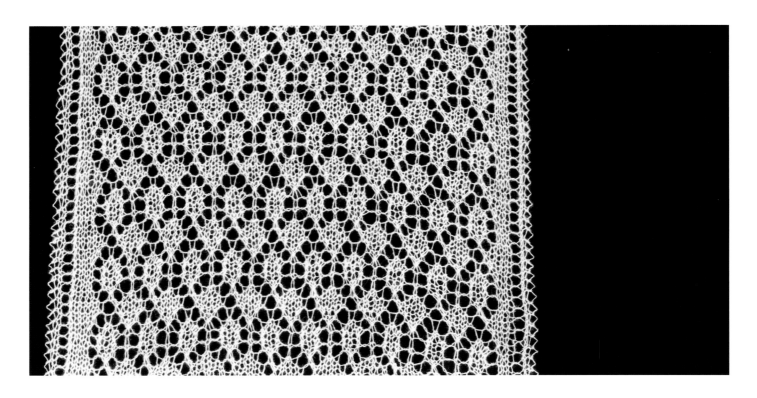

Vaga Scarf chart A

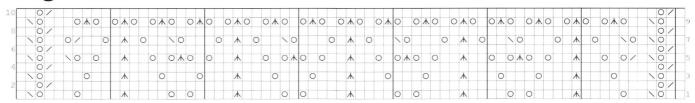

Vaga Scarf chart B

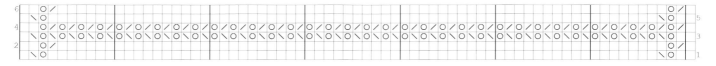

Vaga Scarf chart C

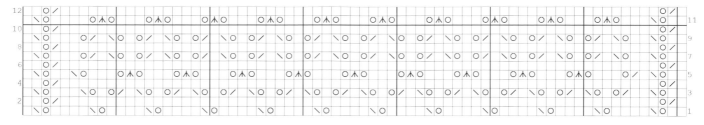

Everything was measured in knuckles (the length of the second finger from tip to knuckle), or span (on a fully stretched hand, distance between the point of the thumb and the point of the little finger). This saved time getting a tape measure.

Quarff Triangular Stole

Designed and knitted by Pearl Johnson. This was designed twenty years ago as an experiment to see how traditional patterns would fit into a non-traditional shape. It is a shawl which is suitable as a shoulder shawl especially for evening wear. Pearl named this triangular stole after the village of Quarff where she grew up.

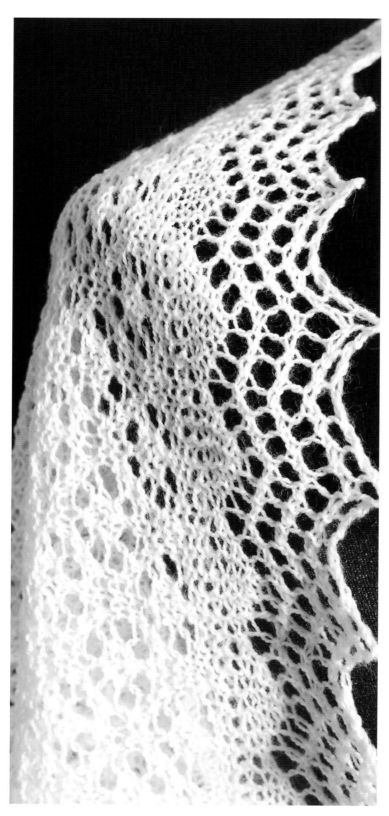

Pearl Johnson

Pearl was taught to knit by her mother and three older sisters. By the age of six she was knitting child's mittens to sell in Lerwick shops.

Her favourite quote comes from Aristotle: "pleasure in the job puts perfection in the work". Applying this to her knitting has led her to win many prizes and trophies locally and at the Royal Highland Show in Edinburgh.

As well as demonstrating in Shetland, her expertise in Shetland knitting has led her to travel extensively both in the UK and abroad. She has demonstrated in Germany, Norway and Japan. She also demonstrated knitting to Prince Charles and the late Princess Diana in 1986, and to the Prime Minister of the time.

She passes on her skills through workshops, and visits organised through the Shetland Guild of Spinners, Knitters, Weavers and Dyers. Most of these visitors are American, Japanese, Canadian or Norwegian.

Pearl has won many prizes for her knitting at shows in Shetland, and at the Royal Highland Show in Edinburgh. Pearl regrets that hand knitting is too slow a process to provide a worthwhile income but she does sell some of her knitting through outlets in Lerwick.

She is very glad that this book has been produced by folk living and knitting in Shetland and hopes that it will raise more awareness of Shetland traditional knitting.

Materials:

4 X 25g balls 2ply Shetland Lace Yarn

2 X 3.25 mm (UK 11, USA 3) knitting needles

Tapestry needle for grafting

Markers for separating stitches for each chart

Sizing:

Width 114cm (45ins)

Depth 55cm (21.5ins)

Tension:

24 stitches and 36 rows for 10cm (4ins)

Instructions:

Cast on 8, PM, cast on 1, PM, cast on 8, a total of 17 stitches.

Simultaneously follow chart A for right hand edge, chart B for main part of shawl, chart C for left hand edge.

Work chart A rows 1 to 14 once, rows 15 to 26 eighteen times, rows 15 to 18 once.

Work chart B until row 90 is completed, work rows 75 to 90 another nine times, continuing with increases as set by chart, keeping pattern correct. (233 stitches)

Work chart C rows 1 to 14 once, rows 15 to 26 eighteen times, rows 15 to 18 once.

Now continue:

Chart A Work row 19

Panel B Knit 5, knit 2 together (knit 8, knit 2 together) 22 times, knit 6. (210 stitches)

Chart C Work row 19

Break yarn leaving 10" (26 cm) for grafting with later. Place 12 stitches of chart C on a holder.

Pattern Notes:

This triangular stole is knitted in garter stitch from the bottom up and increased out to the neck edge. The side edges are worked along with the main part of the shawl and right hand edging is continued along and knitted onto the last row of the shawl. The edge peaks have a pattern row repeat of 12 rows (charts A and C) and the main 'cat's paw' pattern has a pattern repeat 16 rows (chart B).

Note; Markers (shown as PM) are placed when casting on to denote the different sections.

Turn work and rejoin yarn at stitch next to holder, knit 210 (chart B) stitches followed by chart A row 20.

Work and attach edging:

Following chart D start to work edging.

At the end of each pattern row knit the last edge stitch together with the adjacent stitch from the top edge of main part of shawl. Continue in this way working chart D rows 1 to 12 thirty four times and once more ending with a row 11.

Note: In row 5 of chart D, you will need to knit 3 together to keep pattern correct and join to main part.

Graft left hand edging (see page 12) and top edging stitches together. Sew cast on stitches together. Weave in ends.

Wash and dress according to instructions on page 15 for this type of garment.

'Kemp' means to vie or strive to be first. Sometimes knitters did kemp to see who could knit most. In other parts of Shetland knitters use the word kemp to knit quickly and with dogged determination to get something finished; this could be to meet a deadline or, in the past, just the need for high volume production to get basic household essentials.

Quarff Triangular Stole

chart C

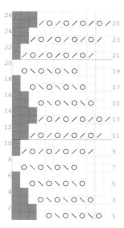

Quarff Triangular Stole

chart A

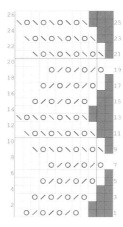

Quarff Triangular Stole chart B

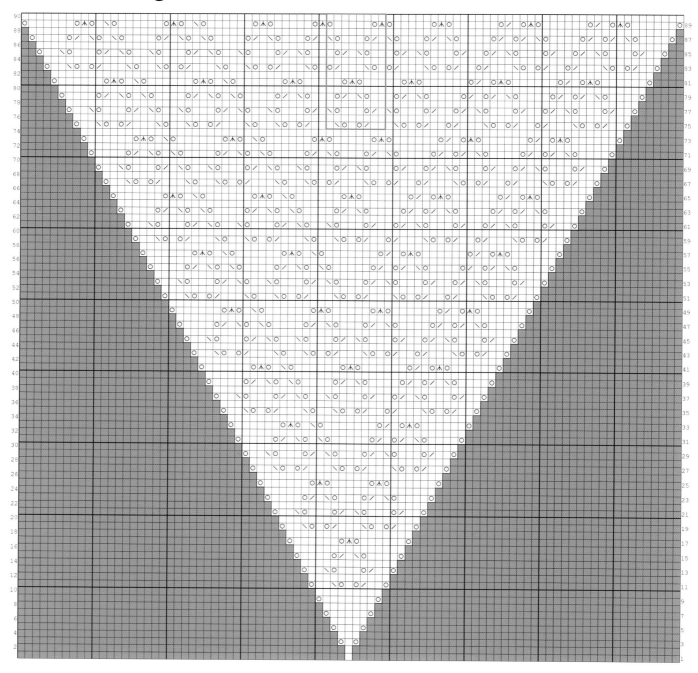

Every household had wooden "boards" for dressing knitting. Adjustable hap and jumper boards as well as various sizes of scarf, glove, mitten and sock boards were all needed. Berets are often dressed on large flat plates, though some have wooden boards for that too.

Quarff Triangular Stole

chart D

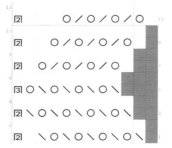

Kirk Ness Scarf

Designed and knitted by Ina Irvine. Ina named this scarf Kirk Ness for two reasons. Part of the scarf reminds her of arched windows in a church or cathedral so Kirk became part of the name. The edging is like a series of headlands; the Shetland word for headland is Ness.

Materials:

2 x 25g ball 100% Shetland 1 ply yarn

2 x 2mm (UK 14, USA 00) knitting needles

Spare needle or stitch holder

Tapestry needle for grafting

Sizing:

Length 104 cm (41 in.)
Width 27 cm (10.5 in.)

Tension:

36 stitches, 60 rows for 10 cm (4 in.)

Pattern Notes:

The entire scarf is knitted in garter stitch (all knit rows) unless otherwise stated. The scarf is knitted in two halves to ensure the end patterns match and is therefore grafted together in the middle.

Note the 2 new symbols in the chart of this scarf:
◉ Stitch 3 on row 1 is a lock stitch following the 2 cast off (bind off) stitches and creates the interesting edging.

The ⊟ sign indicates a purl stitch. Both of these symbols are described in the Chart Symbols on page 10.

Instructions:

Cast on 89 stitches.
Knit 1 plain row.
Follow the chart.
Row 1 read from right hand side. At end of this row the stitch number increases to 91.
Row 2 and all even rows read from left.
Knit to row 58.
Continue the pattern working rows 59 to 78 eleven times.
This completes the first half of the scarf.

Leave these stitches on a spare needle or stitch holder.

Cast on 89 stitches, knit the second half of the scarf exactly the same as the first but omit row 78 on the last repeat.

Graft the two halves together using garter stitch method, taking care not to pull the wool too tightly. See page 12.

Prepare for washing and dressing according to instructions on page 15, including pinning out the ends to emphasise the points.

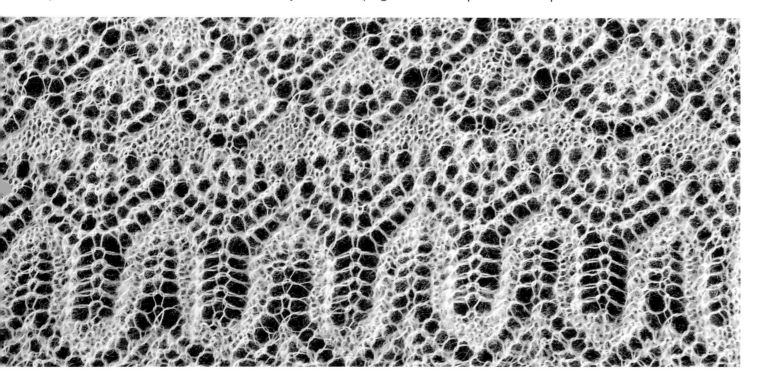

Kirk Ness Scarf chart

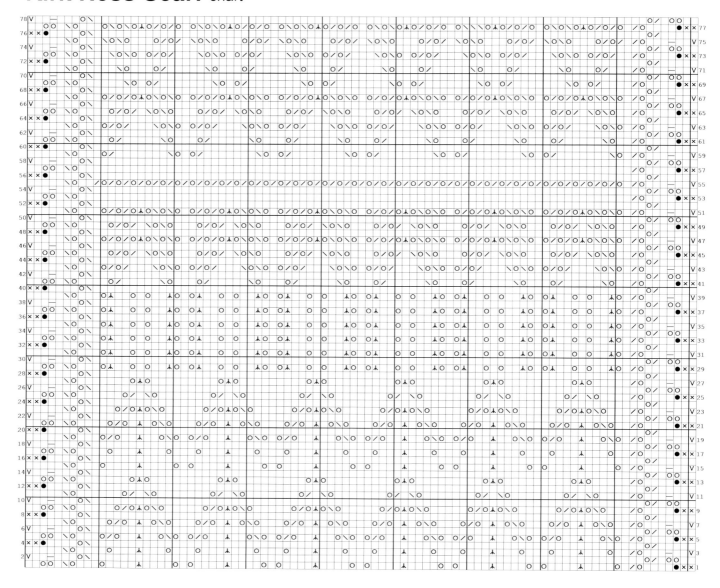

Especially in the 1960s and 1970s thousands of jumpers and cardigans were knitted in Shetland, some plain but many with hand knit Fair Isle or lace yokes. These were exported all over the world. The plain parts of the garments were machine knitted, mostly in family homes by men and women, for one of the local businesses, and provided valuable income. Many youngsters were lulled to sleep by the sound of the knitting machine. The machine knit pieces were distributed to other homes where yokes were knitted, cuffs and necks grafted on and rib seams invisibly joined – this part was known as 'feenishin'. Most of the contributors to this book were involved with some part of this industry.

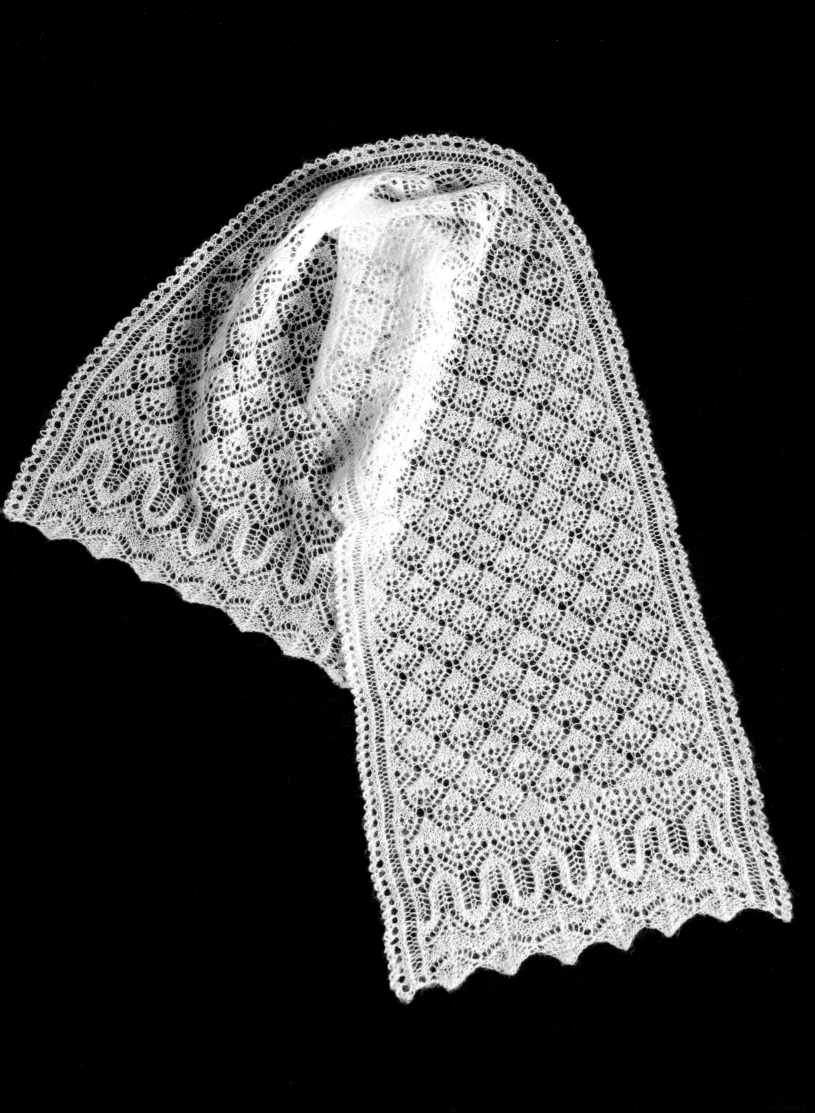

Peerie Bead and Diamond Scarf

This scarf was designed and knitted by Kathleen Anderson. Kathleen used this pattern with students at her lace knitting evening class.

Materials:

1 x 25g ball 100% Shetland 1 ply yarn

2 x 2mm (UK 14, USA 00) knitting needles

Spare needle or stitch holder

Tapestry needle for grafting

Sizing:

Length 127 cm (50 in.)
Width 13 cm (5 in.)

Tension:

44 stitches, 50 rows for 10 cm (4 in.)

Pattern Notes:

This scarf is knitted in garter stitch throughout and does not require grafting. The motifs used are a peerie bead in a diamond over the whole length.

Instructions:

Cast on 55 stitches.

Knit 5 rows.

Start pattern by following the chart starting at row 1 and reading from the right hand side.

This pattern is knitted every row with row 2 and each even number row being read from the left hand side.

Repeat the 10 rows of the pattern for the required length of the scarf and then knit rows 1 to 5.

Knit 5 rows to finish and cast off neatly.

The scarf should then be dressed using the method described on page 15.

Sweerie geng – the first row knitted following cast on. 'Never stop in da middle o a sweerie geng or it will hae bad luck'.

Peerie Bead and Diamond Scarf chart

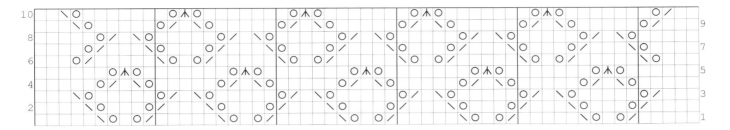

Gairdins Top

Designed by Hazel Tindall. This design, with leaves and trees, is named after 'Da Gairdins', at Sand on the West Mainland of Shetland, which is one of Hazel's favourite places.

Materials:

Jamiesons of Shetland Ultra (50% Shetland/50% Lambswool) 4/5/6/8/10/11 x 25 g

Two 3 mm (UK 11, USA 2) knitting needles or Circular needle 60 cm (24 in.) long

Stitch markers

Stitch holders (optional - threading stitches on a length of cotton in contrasting colour will do just as well)

Thin cotton thread in contrasting colour.

Tapestry needle

Sizing:

	XS	S	M	L	1X	2X
Actual bust:	71 cm	84 cm	97 cm	117 cm	130 cm	145 cm
	28"	33"	38"	46"	51"	57"
Length to back neck:	53 cm	56 cm	59 cm	65 cm	68 cm	71 cm
	21"	22"	23"	25.5"	27"	28"

Tension:

After dressing: 28 sts & 40 rows = 10cm/4" over leaf pattern using 3 mm needles

Abbreviations:

RS	right side	WS	wrong side	yo	yarn over
K2tog	knit two together	K3tog	knit three together	PM	place marker

Pattern Notes:

There are no purl stitches in this pattern.

Garter stich background makes it hard to distinguish right side/wrong side. You may find it helpful to put a coloured thread on the right side of each piece.

Joining the yarn: tie in a loose knot, leaving two long ends. Once the garment is finished, undo the knot, make sure the stitches at either side are not too slack, half tie the knot, separate the strands in each end, then weave each strand separately in four different directions. (More time consuming than weaving ends as you knit, but it is less bulky.)

Sleeves are knitted with no armhole shaping, and flat. If you knit the sleeves first, the exact width is not so crucial and more productive than knitting tension swatches – so you can adjust the body or needle size if needed. Optional – put all stitches on cotton thread, wash and block the sleeves flat; that gives the option to double check tension before starting the body. This also saves the trouble of blocking sleeves at the same time as the body.

Sleeve stitches are used for joining to body's armhole stitches, to the sides of the fronts and back, and for knitting the yoke.

The body, up to armholes, is knit in one piece, with front borders eight stitches wide.

After dropping the armhole stitches, the back and fronts are knit separately until the yoke begins. The back is longer than the fronts to ensure that the neck is lower at the front.

Yoke is knitted in one piece, using stitches from body and sleeves. Row 12 of the leaf pattern is used to join all the stitches for the yoke. The yoke stitches gradually decrease, as indicated on the chart.

An exact fit is not necessary – the wide borders gives the option to have it overlapped, worn edge to edge or slightly apart at the centre front. You could put one or two buttons at the top so that it overlaps.

Gairdins Top chart A

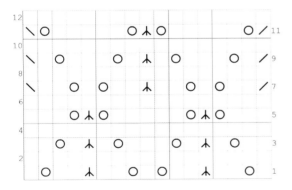

If a tail of yarn is left too long when laying up (using the thumb method), it will be a long time before the item is finished.

Chart A LEAF PATTERN – multiples of 8 stitches + 1, 12 rows, charted instructions included.

Even rows are all knit.

Row 1 (RS): K1, yo, K2 *K3tog, K2, yo, K1, yo, K2 repeat from * to last 6 stitches, K3tog, K2, yo, K1.

Row 3: K2, yo, K1, * K3tog, K1, yo, K3, yo, K1 repeat from * to last 6 stitches, K3tog, K1, yo, K2.

Row 5: K3, yo, * K3tog, yo, K5, yo, repeat from * to last 6 stitches, K3tog, yo, K3.

Row 7: K2tog, K2, yo *K1, yo, K2, K3tog, K2, yo, repeat from * to last 5 stitches, K1, yo, K2, K2tog.

Row 9: K2tog, K1, yo, K1 *K2, yo, K1, K3tog, K1, yo, K1, repeat from * to last 5 stitches, K2, yo, K1, K2tog.

Row 11: K2tog, yo, K2 *K3, yo, K3tog, yo, K2, repeat from * to last 5 stitches, K3, yo, K2tog.

Gairdins Top chart B

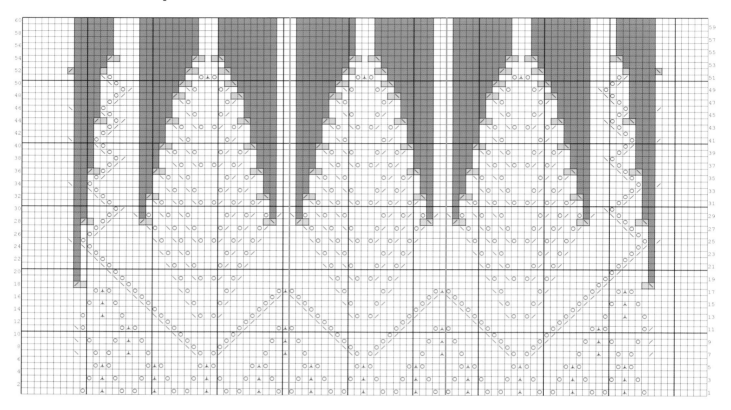

Gairdins Top chart C

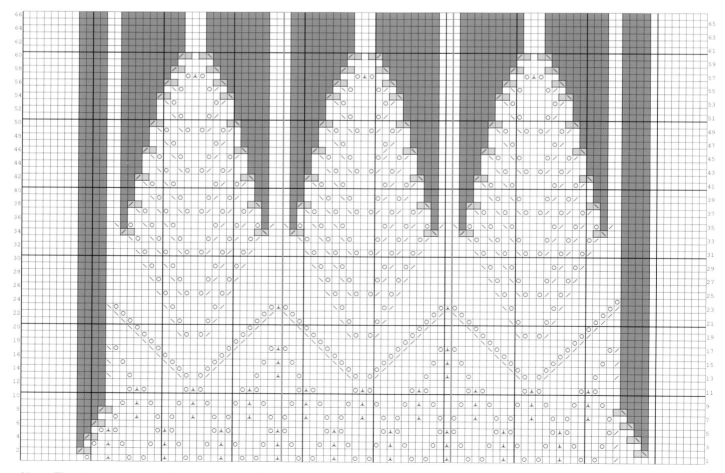

Note: The blue squares indicate the two stitches to be knitted together to give the decreases required to shape the yoke.

Instructions:

RIGHT SLEEVE

Cast on 81 (89, 97,113, 129, 145) stitches.

Row 1 K8 (8, 8, 12, 12, 12), PM, K9, PM, K39 (47, 55, 63, 79, 95), PM, K18, PM, K7 (7, 7, 11, 11, 11). The stitches at the beginning and end of the row will be used to join to the armhole stitches on body. The group of 9 stitches will be used to join to the side of the right front and the 18 stitches will join to the RS of the back. The middle stitches will be used to knit the yoke.

#Rows 2-9: Knit.

Row 10 (RS) onwards, follow instructions/chart A. Work 5 (6, 6, 6½, 7½, 8½) pattern repeats. End last repeat on the 11th (11th, 11th, 5th, 5th, 5th) pattern row. Break the yarn.#

With RS facing you, place first 17 (17, 17, 21, 21, 21) stitches and last 25 (25, 25, 29, 29, 29) stitches onto waste cotton. This leaves the centre 39 (47, 55, 63, 79, 95) stitches for the yoke. Put these on a stitch holder or waste cotton.

LEFT SLEEVE

Repeat instructions for right sleeve * to *.

Row 1 K7 (7, 7, 11, 11, 11), PM, K18, PM, K39 (47, 55, 63, 79, 95), PM, K9, PM, K8 (8, 8, 12, 12, 12).

Repeat instructions for right sleeve # to #.

With RS facing you, place first 25 (25, 25, 29, 29, 29) stitches and last 17 (17, 17, 21, 21, 21) stitches onto waste cotton. This leaves the centre 39 (47, 55, 63, 79, 95) stitches for the yoke. Put these on a stitch holder or waste cotton.

BODY

Cast on 177 (209, 241, 289, 321, 361) stitches.

Rows 1-7: Knit.

Row 8: Knit 8, PM, knit 33 (41, 49, 57, 65, 73), PM, knit 15 (15, 15, 23, 23, 23), PM, knit 65 (81, 97, 113, 129, 153), PM, knit 15 (15, 15, 23, 23, 23), PM, knit 33 (41, 49, 57, 65, 73), PM, knit 8. The markers indicate front borders and armhole stitches.

Row 9 (RS) onwards: Knit 8, follow chart A or written instructions for row 1 of leaf pattern, end with K8.

Knit chart A for 9 (10, 11, 12, 13, 14) repeats (undressed this is approx 28 (30, 33, 36, 39, 42) cm (11, 12, 13, 14, 15, 16 inches) long. After blocking this will measure approx 3 cm (1 in.) more. Adjust number of repeats if you want this longer or shorter. Finish on row 12.

You are now ready to split into 2 fronts and back. Without turning the work slip 41 (49,57,65,73,81), 15 (15,15,23,23,23), 65 (81,97,113,129,153), 15 (15,15,23,23,23) stitches on to 4 stitch holders or waste cotton.

RIGHT FRONT

Turn work. Work 41 (49, 57, 65, 73, 81) stitches, keeping chart A correct, for 2 repeats, ending on the 11th pattern row. Break yarn.

BACK

Join yarn with RS of work facing you, work on 65 (81, 97, 113, 129, 153) stitches, keeping chart A correct, for 3 repeats, ending on the 11th pattern row. Break yarn.

LEFT FRONT

Join yarn with RS of work facing you. Work on 41 (49, 57, 65, 73, 81), keeping chart A pattern correct, for 2 repeats, ending on the 11th pattern row. You will be using this yarn to start knitting the yoke, so don't break it off.

Different ditties were used to help a bairn learning to knit. One was told to 'pit da hens in, gie dem maet, slip dem oot'.

YOKE

Make sure WS of all pieces are facing you. Start at the left front, K41 (49, 57, 65, 73, 81), K39 (47, 55, 63, 79, 95) (left sleeve), K65 (81, 97, 113, 129, 153) (back), K39 (47, 55, 63, 79, 95) (right sleeve), K41 (49, 57, 65, 73, 81) (right front). You should now have 225 (273 ,321, 369, 433, 505) stitches – 8 for each border and 26 (32, 38, 44, 52, 61) pattern repeats. Take a moment to check that you got the sleeves correct – the larger number of stitches on waste cotton should be adjacent to the back. (This is row 12 of chart A)

L, 1X, 2X size only:

Work one repeat (12 rows) of chart A pattern before starting on Row 1 of the yoke pattern.

XS, S, M, L sizes:

Optional – mark the centre of every 3rd leaf to indicate where bottom of wave and tree begin – you should have marked 8 (10, 12, 14) leaves and have 2 leaves at the end.

Follow chart B for the yoke pattern, taking care to start at Row 1.

1X and 2X sizes only

Optional – mark the centre of 2nd then every 3rd leaf to indicate where bottom of wave and tree begin – you should have marked 17 (20) leaves and have 1 leaf at the end.

Follow chart C for the yoke, taking care to start at Row 1.

All sizes:

The number of yoke stitches decreases so that you should have 69 (81, 93, 105, 119, 137) stitches by the end of the chart.

Cast off loosely.

FINISHING ARMHOLES AND SLEEVES

With RS of right sleeve facing, starting where the yoke begins, put the 42 (42, 42, 50, 50, 50) stitches from the waste cotton onto a knitting needle. Using another knitting needle, or the other end of a circular needle, start at the top of the side of the right front, pick up the longer loops between knitted ridges, 15 (15, 15, 23, 23, 23) armhole stitches, and loops on the side of the back to get a total of 43 (43, 43, 51, 51, 51) stitches. Graft together, taking 2 together at centre of armhole on body. Repeat for the left armhole join, reversing the fitting.

Sew side seams of sleeves – whip stitching long loops between the ridges is enough.

FINISHING

Darn in all ends but do not trim. Remove all markers. Follow finishing instructions on page 15.

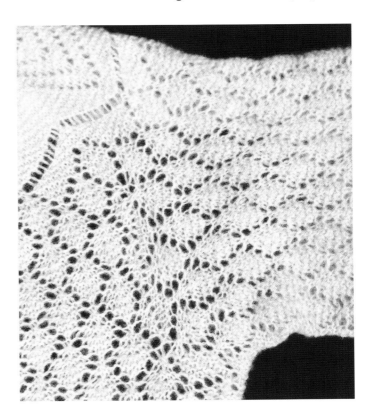

Zig Zag Scarf

Designed and knitted by Zena Thomson. It was the result of an error in knitting the 'new shell' pattern when she was still learning the techniques of lace knitting. She realised an interesting pattern could be achieved by moving the decreases and Zena's Zig Zag pattern was developed.

Materials:

1 x 25 g ball 100% Shetland 1 ply yarn

2 x 3 mm (UK 11, USA 2) knitting needles

Sizing:

Length 118 cm (46 in.)
Width 25 cm (10 in.)

Tension:

30 stitches, 32 rows for 10 cm (4 in.)

Pattern Notes:

This scarf is knitted in garter stitch throughout and does not require grafting. To alter the length of the scarf, adjust by altering the number of repeats of the pattern. The width can be adjusted by adding or subtracting multiples of 8 stitches.

The detail on the long edges of the scarf is locally known by various names, such as 'open stik' or 'love links.'

Instructions:

Cast on 74 stitches.
Knit 1 row.
Follow the chart reading from the right at row 1.
All even numbered rows read from the left.
The 20 rows of the chart form the pattern. Work these rows for the required length of the scarf and finish with rows 1 to 10.
In this case, 19 full repeats plus rows 1 to 10.
Cast off loosely.

Wash carefully and dress according to instructions on page 15 including pinning out the ends to emphasise the points.

Zig Zag Scarf chart

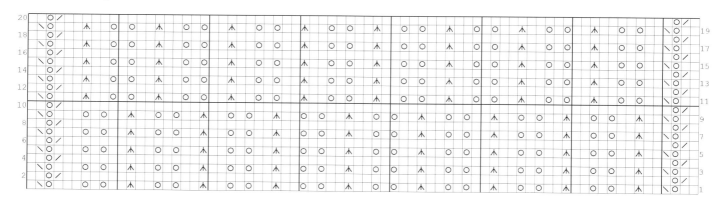

❖ *Fleece could be sent to a spinning mill in Scotland and the desired weight of yarn returned. Zena Thomson also remembers collecting in fleece from customers at a local shop and sending off the bags of wool. One pound of oo (fleece) sent away to be spun gave*
4 hanks of jumper weight yarn
5 hanks of hap yarn
6 hanks of spencer yarn
8 hanks of lace yarn ❖

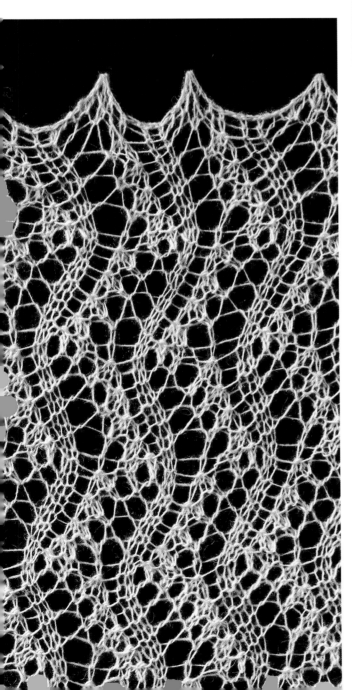

Shoormal Scarf

Designed and knitted by Ina Irvine. Living near the shore and always aware of the sight and sounds of the sea inspired the design and colours for this scarf. The word Shoormal is our term for the water's edge and the high-water mark on the beach. The colours used are natural Shetland colours.

Materials:

1 x 25g ball of 1 ply Shetland Supreme in natural white
1 x 25g ball of 1 ply Shetland Supreme in natural grey
1 x 25g ball of 1 ply Shetland Supreme in natural dark fawn
1 x 25g ball of 1 ply Shetland Supreme in natural moorit
OR
1 x 25g ball of 1 ply Shetland Supreme in one colour

2 x 2 mm (UK14, USA 00) knitting needles
spare needle or stitch holder

Sizing:

Length 100 cm (39 in.)
Width 22 cm (8.5 in.) when dressed

Tension:

38 stitches, 60 rows for 10 cm (4 in.)

Pattern Notes:

The scarf is knitted in garter stitch throughout and is done in two halves, grafted together at the centre.

The narrow edge pattern has a 2 row repeat throughout. The main 20 stitch pattern has an 8 row repeat throughout.

The designer slips the first stitch knitways in every row of this pattern.

When joining a new colour, slip the first stitch knitways, work the next 3 stitches with both colours, leaving the ends to be trimmed after dressing.

*No knitting was done on Sundays.
Knitting was usually done for income
so knitting on the sabbath was frowned
upon. 'Seterday's trift lays aa da week adrift'.
Knitting too late on a Saturday – as the
sabbath approaches – is not a good idea.*

Instructions:

Using grey, cast on 73 stitches loosely.

Knit 1 row.

Reading from the right, follow the chart starting at row 1.

Read even rows from the left.

*Work 16 rows of the chart in grey.

Keeping pattern correct, work 16 rows in dark fawn.

Keeping pattern correct, work 16 rows in moorit.*

Keeping pattern correct, work 16 rows in natural white.

Repeat from * to *. 7 repeats worked.

Join white, work till 29 repeats of chart are complete.

This completes the first half.

Leave these stitches on a spare needle or stitch holder.

Work the second half of the scarf to match the first but finish the pattern at row 15.

Using the method for grafting garter stitch, graft the 2 halves together taking care not to pull the wool too tightly. Instructions can be found on page 12

Wash carefully and dress according to advice on page 15 including pinning out the ends to emphasise the points.

Shoormal Scarf chart

Voxter Scarf

Designed and knitted by Zena Thomson. This scarf is designed and knitted in the traditional style of a Shetland lace scarf having lace edging all round, with a border design at each end and a different design running through the centre. It was designed several years ago by Zena for a weekend workshop, at Voxter House, she was delivering for a WI group.

Materials:
2 X 25 g balls Shetland 1 ply lace yarn
2 X 3 mm (UK 11, USA 2) knitting needles
spare needle

Sizing:
Length 116 cm (46 in.)
Width 30 cm (12 in.)

Tension:
28 stitches, 40 rows for 10 cm (4 in.)

Pattern Notes:

This scarf is knitted in garter stitch throughout. A lace edging is knitted first to form the end of the scarf. After picking up the stitches as described in instructions, the edging is carried on throughout the scarf as can be seen on the charts.

The scarf has been designed so that it can be knitted right through and therefore no grafting is required.

The edging pattern is known by Zena as 'da peerie tree' edging and the border starts with the 'trees' followed by 'da peerie bead' pattern and to finish the border, the diamond pattern. In the centre Zena has used the 'zig zag' she designed for another scarf.

Voxter Scarf chart A

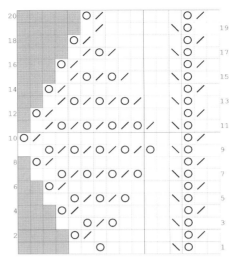

A scalloped edging is 'da lace'.

Voxter Scarf chart B

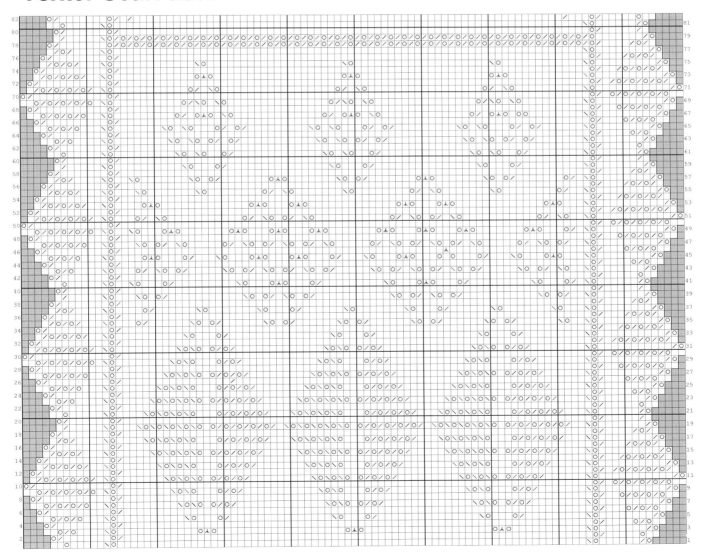

Voxter Scarf chart C

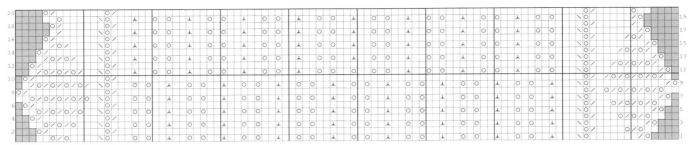

Instructions:

To knit this scarf, start with the lace edging.

Cast on 11 stitches with waste wool and knit 1 row. Join on the main yarn and knit 1 row.

Continue by following chart A reading from the right hand side at row 1. Row 2 and all even rows read from the left hand side.

The 20 rows of this chart complete one pattern. Work until a total of 7 patterns (7 peaks) are done, ending with a row 19.

Leave these 11 stitches on the needle with yarn attached. With a spare needle pick up 67 stitches (the long loops) along the side of the completed lace edging.

Return to the lace edging and knit across these 67 stitches as shown on Row 1 of chart B.

Remove the waste wool row from the cast on end of the lace edging and pick up these 11 stitches on a spare needle.

Now complete row 1 on chart A by knitting these 11 stitches as shown on row 1 of chart A (K2, o, K2tog, K5, o, k2).

Continue chart B starting at row 2 reading from the left. All even rows read from the left hand side, odd numbered rows reading from the right.

Work chart B noting in last row (row 82) the 2 decreases in centre section which are

required to achieve correct number of stitches for centre pattern in chart C.

Now start chart C, work rows 1 to 20 eight times in total.

Now work chart D, noting the increases in row 2 which will restore the stitch count to accommodate the end pattern. Work to row 79. This is the last row to work both side edgings.

Row 80, follow chart at left side then knit across 69 stitches and turn.

Row 81, knit 70 stitches and follow chart at left side.

Row 82 Start to attach edging as follows and as shown on chart.

Work edging as shown, when reaching the ☑ symbol slip the last edge stitch, knit the first stitch from the main part, pass the slipped stitch over the knitted stitch. Turn work and purl the first stitch and continue with edge as charted.

Work chart edging until there are 7 peaks and all main part stitches have been used up.

Graft together the remaining 11 stitches on each needle using the garter stitch grafting instructions. (page 12).

Finish according to instructions on page 15.

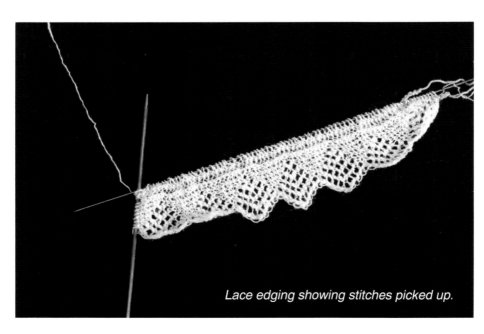

Lace edging showing stitches picked up.

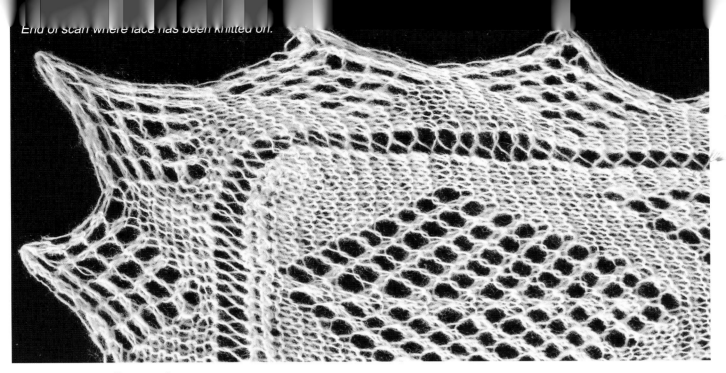

Voxter Scarf chart D

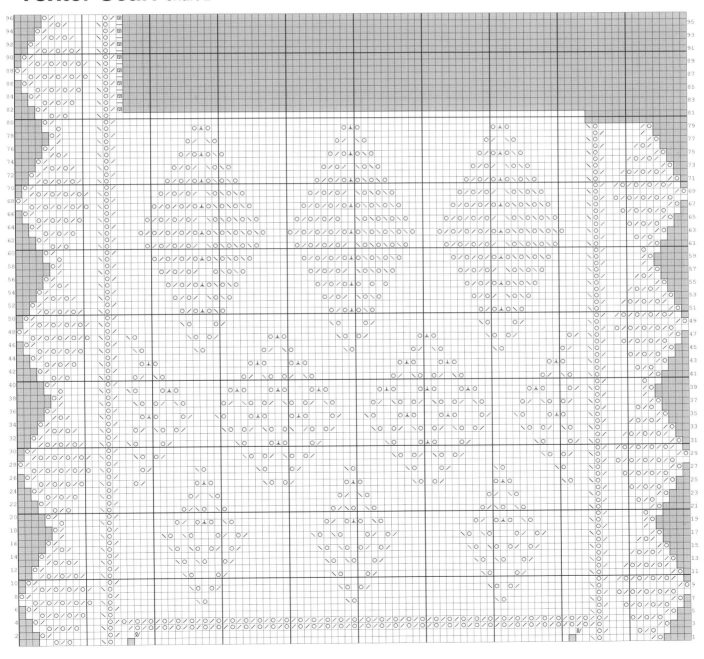

Ringlet Scarf

Designed and knitted by Mary Kay. This scarf was designed a number of years ago for a lace knitting workshop for visitors from Canada. When looking at the lines in the middle of the scarf, Mary's thought was "ringlet", a Shetland word for striped so naming this scarf was easy.

Materials:
2 x 25 g balls 2 ply Shetland lace
yarn or similar

2 x 3 mm (UK 11, USA 2) knitting needles

Stitch holder or extra needle

Tapestry needle for grafting

Sizing:
Length 126 cm (49.5 in.)
Width 18 cm (7 in.)

Tension:
24 stitches, 38 rows for 10 cm (4 in.)

Pattern Notes:

This scarf is knitted in garter stitch and in two halves. The two parts are grafted together using the method described on page 12 for garter stitch.

When knitting ☐☐ as shown on chart in the centre pattern of the end design, keep yarn taut, otherwise a too large lace hole will appear.

Instructions:

Start by casting on 3 stitches.
Increase 1 stitch at each end of every row by knitting twice into the first stitch and second last stitch until there are 45 stitches.

Now follow chart.
Row 1 read from right hand side.
Row 2 and all even rows read from left.
Complete chart to row 75.
Work rows 66 to 75 another 14 times, so there are altogether 15 groups of these 10 rows.
Set aside on a spare needle or stitch holder.

Work the second half of the scarf exactly the same as the first but omit row 75 on the last repeat. Complete the scarf by grafting the two halves together using the garter stitch graft. (Page 12). Dress the scarf according to the instructions on page 15.

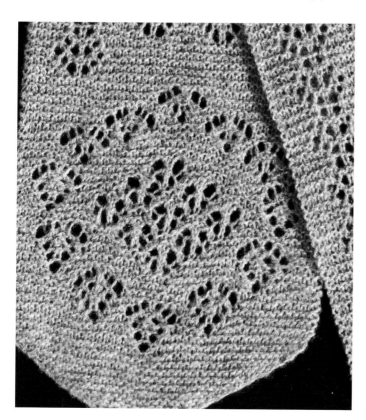

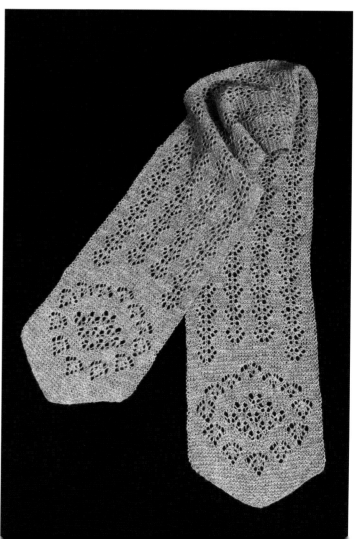

Ringlet Scarf

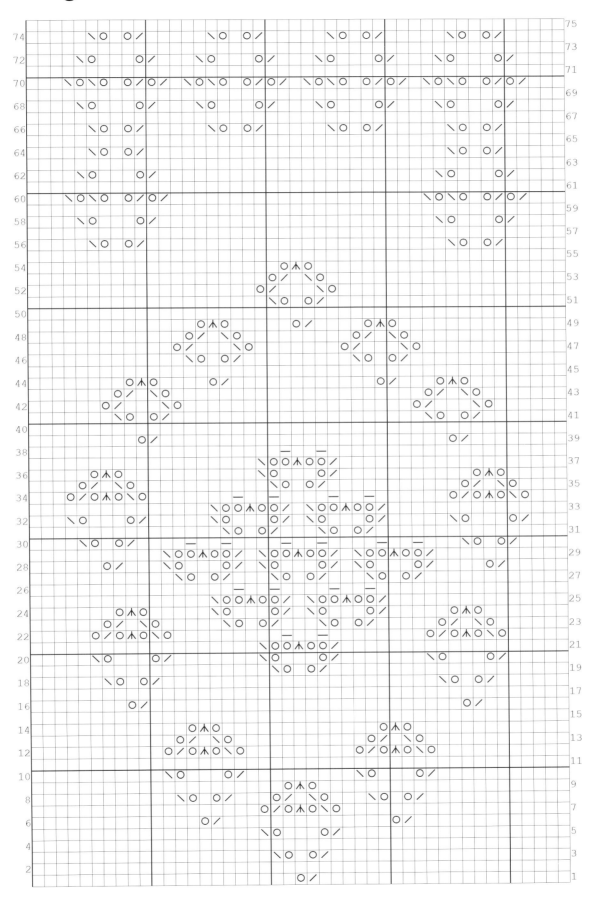

Laureya Cardigan

Designed by Lauretta Robertson. Named after Lauretta's grand-daughters.

Materials:

100% Shetland wool, lace weight 7/9/11/13/15 x 25g

Two 2.25 mm (UK 13, USA 0) knitting needles or circular needle (for body ribs)

Two 3 mm (UK 11, USA 2) knitting needles or circular needle (for body)

Three or four 2.25 mm needles or circular needle (for sleeve)

Three or four 3 mm needles or circular needle (for sleeve)

Buttons 7/7/8/8/8

Stitch markers

Stitch holders (optional - threading stitches on a length of cotton in contrasting colour will do just as well)

Thin cotton thread in contrasting colour.

Tapestry needle

Sizing:

	S	M	L	1X	2X
Bust:	74cm	89cm	104 cm	119cm	135cm
	29"	35"	41"	47"	53"
Length to back neck:	56 cm	61 cm	69 cm	74 cm	79 cm
	22"	24"	27"	29"	31"
Armhole to cuff	46cm	48cm	51cm	53cm	56cm
	18"	19"	20"	21"	22"
Hem to armhole	35.5cm	41cm	45.5cm	48cm	51cm
	14"	16"	18"	19"	20"
Armhole to shoulder	20cm	20cm	23cm	25.5cm	28cm
	8"	8"	9"	10"	11"

Tension:

After dressing: 30 stitches & 38 rows = 10 cm (4 in.) over pattern using 3 mm needles.

Lauretta Robertson

Lauretta was taught to knit by her mother and aunt at four years old. By age fourteen she was knitting lace scarves for sale in the Lerwick shops.

She was employed in Aurora knitwear factory in Walls for a time. This involved examining knitting received from home workers, making repairs if necessary, labelling, brushing, packing and despatching completed garments to customers – at that time most of their buyers were in France.

When she left to have her children she knitted each one a hap and other baby clothes. She continued to knit items for sale from home when her children were young. She mainly knits for her family now and has passed her knitting skills on to them. Recently her three-year-old grand-daughter knitted, with some help, a pair of mittens for her baby sister.

Lauretta is a beautiful knitter and innovative designer who enjoys making haps and scarves, usually designing and adapting her own patterns to suit the item she's making. She has won many prizes and trophies for her knitting in Shetland at Agricultural shows, the annual Guild show, Scottish Women's Royal Institute competitions, and at the Royal Highland Show in Edinburgh. One of Lauretta's furthest travelled pieces is a bridal hat commissioned by a New Zealander.

Lauretta hopes this book will inspire others to learn about Shetland lace knitting and keep the skills alive.

Laureya Cardigan

Abbreviations:

CO	cast on	PM	place marker	RS	right side
WS	wrong side	yo	yarn over	m1	make 1 (increase)
K2tog	knit two together	P2tog	purl two together		
K3tog	slip 1, k2tog, pass slipped stitch over				

PATTERN – multiples of 12 stitches + 1, 10 rows, charted instructions included.

Row 1:   K2tog *K4, yo, K1, yo, K4, K3tog, repeat from *, end K2tog instead of K3tog.

Row 2, 4, 6, 8:   Purl

Row 3:   K2tog *K3, yo, K3, yo, K3, K3tog, repeat from *, end K2tog instead of K3tog.

Row 5:   K2tog *K2, yo, K1 yo, K3tog, yo, K1, yo, K2, K3tog, repeat from *, end K2tog instead of K3tog.

Row 7:   K2tog *K1, yo, K7, yo, K1, K3tog, repeat from *, end K2tog instead of K3tog.

Row 9:   K2tog * yo, K1, yo, K3tog, repeat from *, end K2tog instead of K3tog.

Row 10: Knit (this gives a purl ridge on the right side).

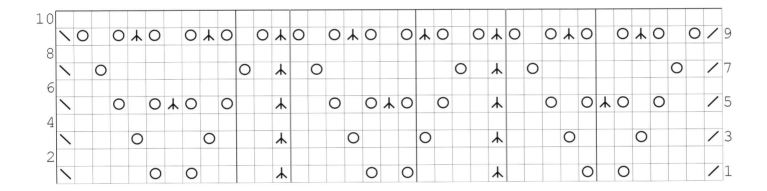

Design notes:

- The body, up to armholes, is knit in one piece, with front borders in moss stitch.
- Buttonholes are worked in rows 3 and 4 and then every 24 [28, 28, 26, 26] rows.
- Optional – place markers 13 stitches from start and finish of row to indicate borders.
- After dropping the armhole stitches, the back and fronts are knit separately.
- Decreases for V neck start after armhole stitches are dropped.
- Work decreases at sides of V neck in even rows of pattern.
- Apart from leaving stitches for under arm, there is no armhole shaping.
- There is no shoulder shaping.
- The back neck moss stitch border is knitted by continuing the right front border, knitting together with one back neck stitch as you go. It is then grafted to the left front border.
- Sleeves are knitted in the round from the cuff up, then grafted to the body. When knitting in the round, remember to knit all stitches in rows 2, 4, 6 and 8 and purl row 10.
- You could omit the ribs to give scalloped edges. If you do that, start with 6 rows of garter stitch (knit every row) between the stitch markers before starting the pattern (2 rows after the first buttonhole has been made).

Instructions:

BODY

Using size 2.25mm needles, CO13, PM, CO192 [240, 288, 336, 384], PM, CO13 stitches.
Total number of stitches: 218 [266, 314, 362, 410]

Row 1: *K1, P1, repeat from *.

Row 2: (P1, K1), 6 times, P1, *P1, K1, repeat from * till second marker, (K1, P1) 6 times, K1.

Row 3 (RS): (K1, P1) 3 times, K1, yo, K2tog, P1, *K1, P1, repeat from *.

Row 4: Work the same as row 2 until you reach yo made in row 3, P1 K1 into yo, P2tog, (K1, P1) twice, K1. First buttonhole has been knitted. Repeat rows one and two till ribs are 28 [32, 32, 32, 32] rows.
Repeat rows 2 and 3, to work a second buttonhole, at the same time increasing one stitch in last row. 219 [267, 315, 363, 411] stitches.
Change to size 3mm needles. Keeping moss stitch borders correct follow written instructions for pattern or chart. Remember to work buttonholes 24 [28, 28, 26, 26] rows after the last one. Work pattern for 12 [14,16,17,18] repeats. The last buttonhole should be in the final pattern repeat.
Adjust number of repeats if you want this longer or shorter.
Note: If you do adjust length you may need to make one more buttonhole between armhole and start of decreases for the V neck.

RIGHT FRONT

Work 13 border stitches + 37 [49, 61, 73, 85] pattern stitches, slip next 23 stitches

BACK
Keeping pattern correct, join yarn with RS of knitting facing you, work next 73 [97, 121, 145, 169] stitches from stitch holder, spare circular needle or cotton thread. Work 8 [8, 9, 10, 10] pattern repeats, omitting row 10 of the last repeat. Break yarn. Put stitches on stitch holder or cotton thread.
From remaining stitches, slip next 23 stitches (for under arm) onto stitch holder or cotton thread.

LEFT FRONT
Work on remaining stitches – this should be 37 [49, 61, 73, 85] pattern stitches + 13 border stitches. Follow instructions for right front from # to #. Break yarn, leaving it long enough to graft shoulder stitches.

SHOULDERS
Put moss stitch border stitches on stitch holders. Divide the back neck stitches so you have 23 [30, 42, 48, 54] for each shoulder. Leave centre 27 [37, 37, 49, 61] stitches on stitch holder, spare circular needle or cotton thread.
Put shoulder stitches on knitting needles. With <u>wrong sides</u> together, graft shoulder stitches, using stocking stitch graft. (Page 12).

BORDER
Put back neck stitches on spare needle. Pick up right front border stitches. #Keeping moss stitch pattern correct, work 12 stitches, knit final stitch together with one stitch from back neck. Turn and moss stitch 13 stitches. Repeat from # until all back neck stitches have been worked. Graft to moss stitch left border. (Page 12 for instruction).

on stitch holder or cotton thread (these will be used when attaching the sleeves). Remaining stitches can be put on stitch holder, spare circular needle or cotton thread.
Keeping pattern correct work one pattern repeat. Now start decreasing for V neck: immediately after working moss stitch decrease one

stitch every 4th row until there are 23 [30, 42, 48, 54] pattern stitches, plus 13 border stitches. Work a total of 8 [8, 9, 10, 10] pattern repeats from armhole to shoulder. Keep stitches on stitch holder or cotton thread.# Leave long length of wool – this will be used to make the border which goes round the back neck.

SLEEVES

Using size 2.25 mm needles, cast on 54 [60, 68, 78, 86] stitches. Join to work in the round.

Row 1: *K1, P1, repeat from *. PM at end of row.

Repeat till rib is 46 rows.

Increase row:

S K1, m1, (K3, m1) to last 2 stitches, K1, m1, K1 – 73 stitches

M K1, m1, (K2, m1, K3, m1) to last 4 stitches, K2, m1, K1, m1, K1 – 85 stitches

L K1, m1, (K2, m1, K3, m1) to last 2 stitches, K1, m1, K1, m1 – 97 stitches

1X K2, m1, (K2, m1, K3, m1) to last 1 stitch, K1– 109 stitches

2X K1, m1, (K2, m1, K3, m1) to last 5 stitches, K2, m1, K1, m1, K1 – 121 stitches

Change to size 3 mm needles.

Follow written or chart instructions to match the body – as you are knitting in the round all stitches in rows 1 to 9 are knit; only the stitches in row 10 are purled.

Increase every 6th row - one stitch at beginning and end of row. Easiest is probably in even row of pattern. Added stitches should be worked in pattern when possible.

Stop increases once you have 121 [133, 145, 157, 169] stitches. Continue without shaping till 15 [16, 17, 18, 19] repeats, omitting row 10 of last repeat. Do not break yarn.

ATTACHING SLEEVES

Pick up stitches for the armhole from the body and underarm stitches. Check number of stitches picked up. Calculate how many extra stitches are on the sleeve. Purl one row on the sleeve, decreasing evenly so that stitch numbers on body and sleeve match. Graft sleeve to body. Take care to align the centre of under arm stitches with the end of sleeve row marker. Repeat for second sleeve.

FINISHING AND DRESSING

Weave in all ends but do not trim. Remove all markers. Follow finishing instructions on page 15.

Wintertime, especially, used to be enlivened by visiting neighbours 'aboot da night'. Women always took their knitting with them on such visits, and many inches were knitted as they caught up on all the local news. It was also a chance to see what others were knitting and exchange ideas.

Simmer Dim Scarf

Designed by Winnie Balfour. The idea for the design of this scarf came from the yarn used. Hanks of white lace yarn were random dyed at a workshop with a friend and the colours obtained resembled the colours of the 'simmer dim' (the twilight of a Shetland summer evening). To retain the variety of colour, it was decided to design a simple pattern using stocking stitch.

Winnie Balfour

At about age five and recovering from whooping cough, Winnie was taught to 'cast a loop' by a neighbour living in the flat below, in Lerwick. At that time there was a keen demand for hand knitted goods. She can recall being fascinated by the row of plates covered with Fair Isle berets, knitted by her mother, drying on the mantelpiece and waiting to be sold. Her first knitting was probably a doll's scarf but she can remember at an early age being allowed to knit the plain garter rows in spencers and haps being knitted by her aunts.

As in most Shetland households, there was always knitting to supplement the income. It was part of life and her mother never sat 'haand idle'. Knitting skills were absorbed without really being aware of it. She remembers learning by having instructions dictated and demonstrated to her rather than by using written patterns. She learned to knit simple Fair Isle and aged eleven was very pleased to be able to sell the children's Fair Isle mittens she had knitted to Tulloch's of Shetland for 2/6 a pair.

As an adult, she knitted for herself and her family and, as was customary with many Shetland girls at that time, knitted for her future husband!

When she joined the Guild of Spinners, Knitters, Weavers, and Dyers, she was keen to learn to spin a finer yarn and became more interested in lace knitting. She was very impressed by the skill of so many Guild members in fine lace knitting and aware of the risk of losing these skills and this very important part of our heritage. It was obvious some effort needed to be made to preserve it and pass it on and this became her main interest.

She hopes that this book may encourage young knitters to take an interest in and enjoy learning, developing and continuing the skills of the legacy we have been left.

Materials:
2 x 25 g balls Shetland Lace weight yarn

2 x 3 mm (UK 11, USA 2) knitting needles

Sizing:
Length variable according to pattern repeats
Width 19 cm (7.5 in.)

Tension:
34 stitches, 36 rows for 10 cm (4in.)

Pattern Notes:

This scarf is knitted in Shetland lace weight yarn. It is knitted in stocking stitch throughout except along the edges as described in instructions.

Instructions:

Cast on 3 stitches and knit 1 row.

Follow chart A starting at row 1 by knitting twice into first stitch and second stitch(5 sts)

Row 2 Knit

Row 3 Increase by knitting twice into first stitch and second last stitch as shown on chart (7 sts)

Row 4 Knit

Row 5 Start of pattern as shown on chart (K3, yo, K1, yo, K3)

Row 6 Knit 3 purl to last 3 sts, then knit 3

Follow the chart and note that each alternate row, e.g. row 8, 10, etc. is K3, purl to last 3 sts. then K3

Repeat row 53 to 68 on the chart for the length required for the scarf.

Start the decreasing according to chart B maintaining the diamond pattern as shown.

To finish scarf, cast off the 5 stitches left on the needle.

Wash and dress carefully according to the instructions on page 15, pinning out the ends to maintain the shape.

Make tassels and attach as shown if desired.

Simmer Dim Scarf chart A

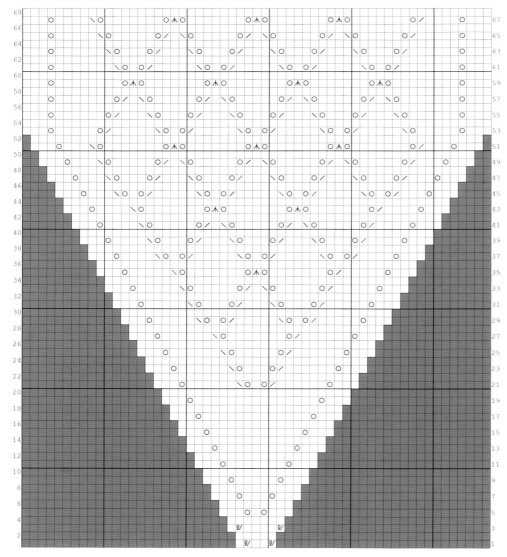

Simmer Dim Scarf chart B

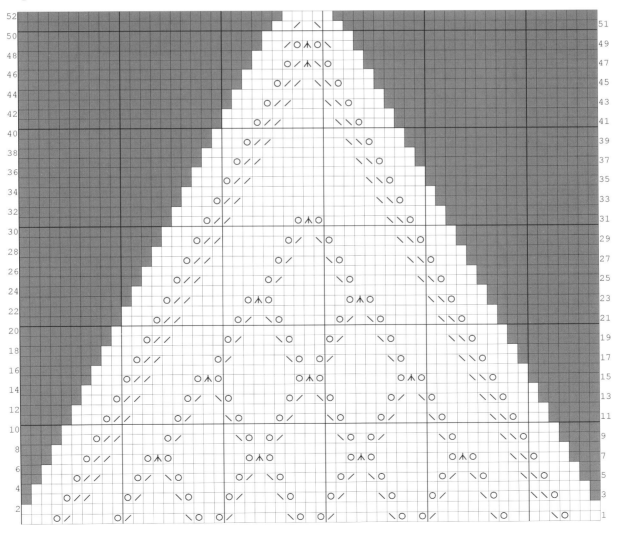

Gilda Scarf

Adapted and knitted by Zena Thomson. This scarf is in memory of Gilda Johnson from Unst, an expert spinner and lace knitter, who was a guild member for several years. Following Gilda's sudden death, her mother donated some of Gilda's lace knitting patterns to Shetland Guild of Spinners, Knitters, Weavers and Dyers for them to use. Zena Thomson has adapted one of these for this scarf.

Materials:
2 x 25g balls 1 ply Shetland lace yarn
2 x 3 mm (UK 11, USA 2) knitting needles
Spare needle

Sizing:
Length 110 cm (43 in.)
Width 37 cm (15 in.)

Tension:
24 stitches, 38 rows for 10cm (4ins)

Pattern Notes:
This scarf is knitted in garter stitch throughout. A lace edging is knitted first to form the end of the scarf. After picking up the stitches as described in instructions, the edging is carried on throughout the scarf as can be seen on the charts. The scarf is knitted in two parts and grafted together.

Gilda called the edging pattern 'da single diamond lace wi peerie chain'. The border patterns, in the sequence they are used are: 'lacey holes', 'roaches', 'lacey holes', 'spider's web', 'lacey holes'. The middle patterns are 'draps' and 'madeira patches'. You may find it useful to place markers.

Instructions:
To knit this scarf, start with the lace edging.
*Cast on 14 stitches with waste wool and knit 1 row. Join on the main yarn and knit 1 row.
Continue by following chart A reading from the right at row 1. Row 2 and all even rows read from the left.
The 12 rows of this chart complete one pattern and are repeated until a total of 11 patterns (11 peaks) ending with a row 12 are done.
Leave these 14 stitches on the needle with yarn attached.
Remove the waste wool row from the cast on end of the lace edging. Using a second needle, pick up these 14 stitches and then pick up 66 stitches (the long loops) along the straight side of the completed lace edging.
Return to the 14 stitches where yarn is attached. Work chart B.*

Work chart C rows 1 to 36 five times in total. Work rows 1 to 11. Keep stitches on needle and leave long thread.

Knit second part to match the first from * to * but omit the last row of chart B.

Graft two pieces together using garter stitch graft. (Page 12).

Finish following instructions on page 15.

Gilda Scarf started and knitting belt lying near by.

When laying up, measure yarn from forefingers to elbow – that length will be enough to cast on about 30 stitches using jumper weight yarn.

Gilda Scarf chart A

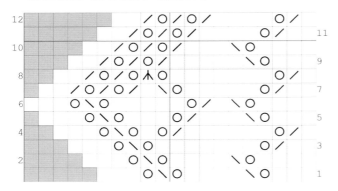

Gilda Scarf chart B

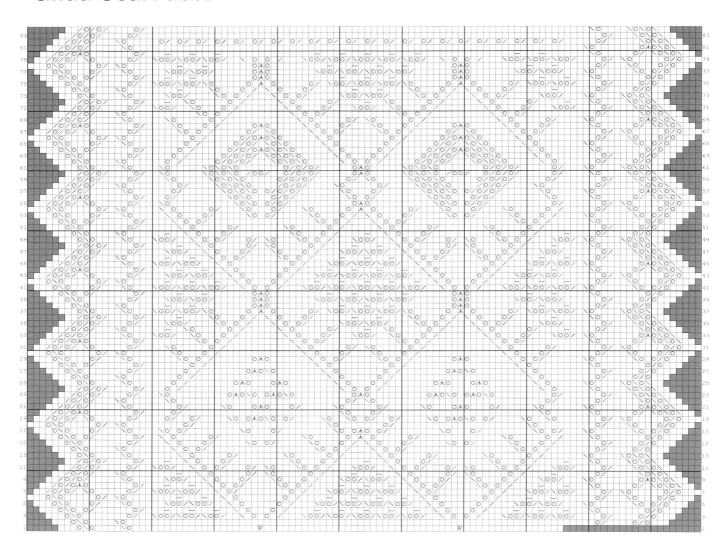

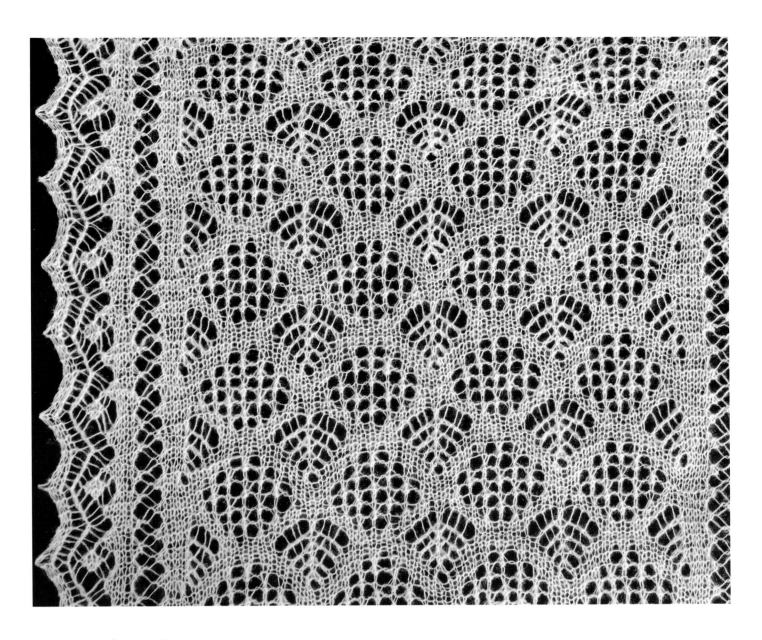

Gilda Scarf chart C

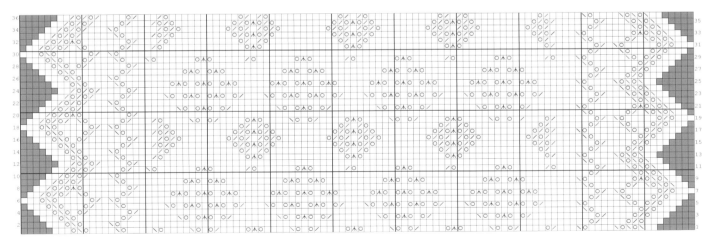

St Ringan's Scarf

Designed and knitted by Mary Kay. This pattern, with bells forming the main motif in the two borders of the design was a reminder of a church, St Ringan's, in Lerwick, now the Public Library. The scarf was knitted in Shetland hand spun yarn but the equivalent weight is suggested. St Ringan's is the old name for St Ninian's isle.

Materials:

2 x 25g balls 100% Shetland 1 ply yarn

2 x 2.75 mm (UK 12, USA 1) knitting needles

Spare needle or stitch holder

Tapestry needle for grafting

Sizing:

Length 90 cm (36 in.)
Width 25 cm (10 in.)
after dressing

Pattern Notes:

This scarf is knitted in two sections and then grafted together. The borders have a central design of bells framed by cat's paw motifs. The triangular shapes are formed by a motif known as 'fancy net'.

The placing of the delayed decreases in the bells pattern creates the shape. The centre design consists of Madeira and Diamond motifs.

Instructions:

Cast on 79 stitches.

Knit 8 rows.

Follow chart A until the 85 rows of pattern have been completed.

Knit 1 row.

Leave on a spare needle or stitch holder and set aside.

Start again casting on 79 stitches.

Knit 8 rows and then 85 rows of chart A. Continue with 3 knit rows.

Follow chart B for middle pattern knitting these 56 rows.

Knit these 56 rows another 3 times making 4 completed patterns.

To complete the centre of the scarf, knit the first 16 rows of chart B again, so that the last row of the pattern is a knit row.

This is designed so that the end of the centre section matches (almost but not quite) the beginning.

The two sections of the scarf are now ready to be grafted together using the garter stitch graft, see page 12.

Instructions for finishing are found on page 15.

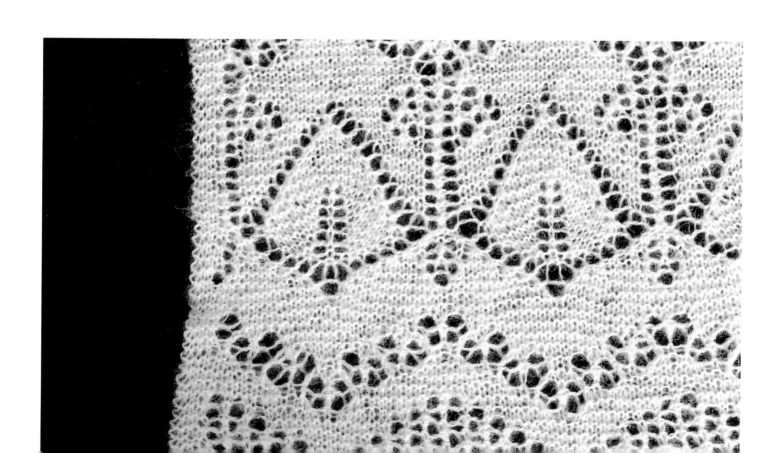

St Ringan's Scarf chart A

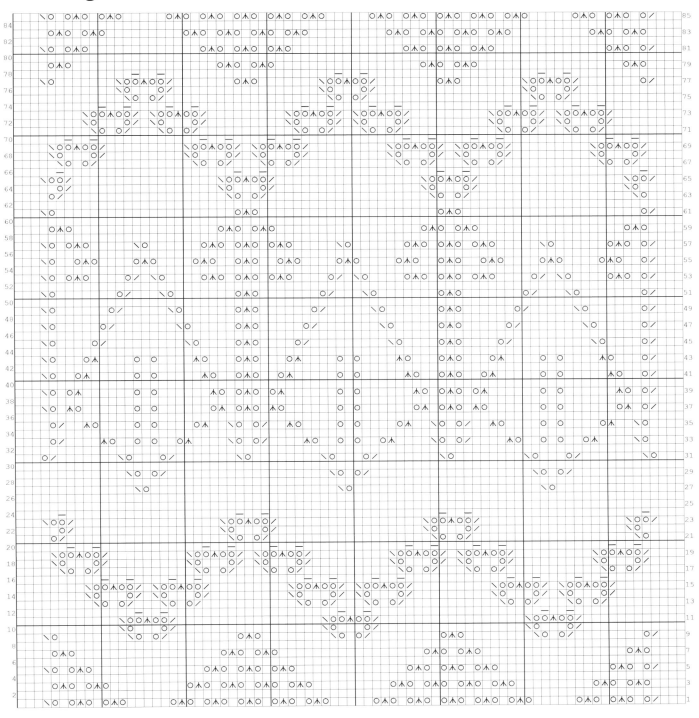

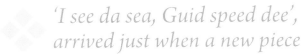

*'I see da sea, Guid speed dee', said by a visitor who
arrived just when a new piece of knitting was starting.*

A raepin string is a strong cotton thread used to draw together the end of the knitting, giving it a long tail which is either sat on, wound around a knitting belt or pinned to the back of the knitter's clothing. This creates tension and helps increase knitting speed. With one part of the knitting secured in a raepin string and the needles stuck in a belt, the knitter is 'hands free' to tend to other household chores (cooking, stoking the fire etc) in between bouts of knitting.

St Ringan's Scarf chart B

Shelley Scarf

Designed by Lauretta Robertson. This scarf is knitted using the very popular cockle shell pattern. The written instructions look complicated but everything is much clearer once you start knitting. Like many things in the knitting world, there are different ways of knitting this pattern. This scarf is named after the main pattern, the cockle shell.

Materials:

3 x 25g balls of 100% Shetland wool, 2 ply lace weight

Two 2.5 mm (UK 12, USA 1) knitting needles

Stitch holder, or a spare knitting needle

Tapestry needle

Sizing:

Sizes are approximate as it will depend on dressing.
Instructions are given for a scarf which is 4 cockles wide and has 15 repeats in each half.
This gives a scarf which is approximately 26 cm (10½ in.) wide and 100 cm (39 in.) long

Tension:

Each cockle is approx 6.5 cm wide and 3 cm high using 2.5 mm needles

Abbreviations:

yo   yarn over
K2tog   knit two together

Pattern Notes:

The scarf is knitted in two halves and grafted together at the middle.

Every row starts with a yarn over – this makes dressing easier and gives the scarf scalloped sides.

Except for the last stitch on the row, knit and purl into every yarn over made in the previous row.

Stitch numbers increase in rows 4 and 8.

Pattern uses multiples of 19 stitches plus four. Instructions given are for 4 repeats.

Changing yarn colours emphasises the shape.

You may find it useful to put a coloured thread on either the right or wrong side of the scarf (row 1 is the wrong side).

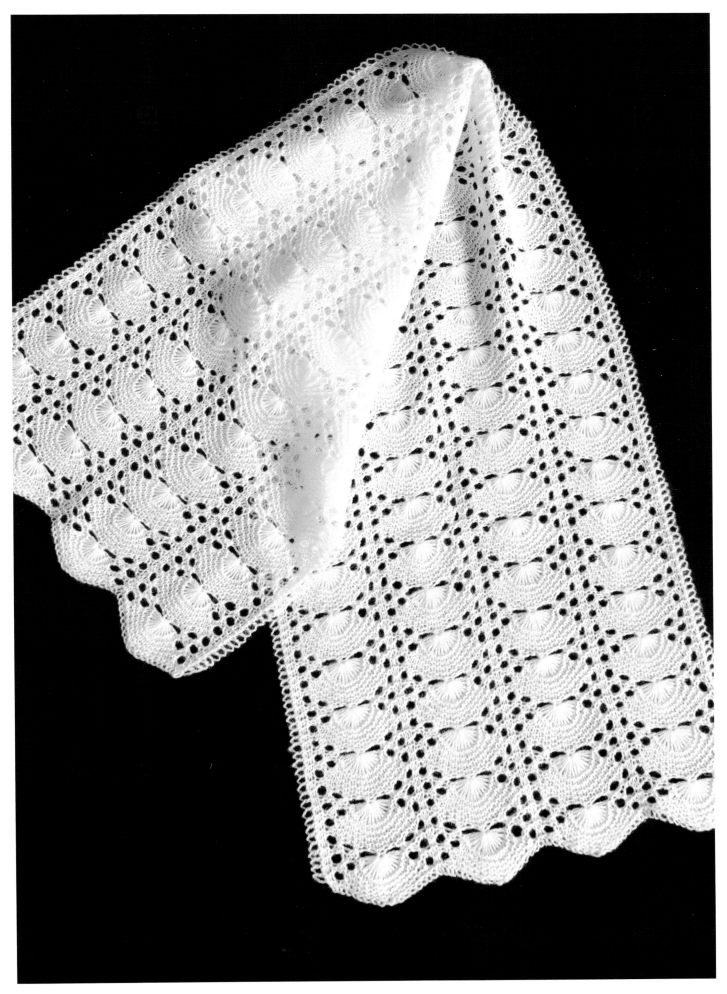

Instructions:

Loosely cast on 80 stitches, using size 2.5 mm needles

Rows 1, 2, 5, 6, 9:   yo, K2 tog, knit to end.

Row 3:   yo, K2tog, K1, *yo, K2tog, K13, K2tog, yo, K2, repeat from *, end K1.

Row 4:   yo, K2tog, K1, *(K1, P1 into yo), K15, *(K1, P1 into yo), K2, repeat from *, end K1 (21 stitches in each repeat).

Row 7:   yo, K2tog, K1 *(yo, K2tog) twice, K11, (K2tog, yo) twice, K2, repeat from *, end K1.

Row 8:   yo, K2tog, K1 *(K1, P1 into yo), K1, (K1, P1 into yo), K13, (K1, P1 into yo), K1, (K1, P1 into yo), K2, repeat from *, end K1. (25 stitches in each repeat).

Row 10:   yo, K2tog, K1, *K5, K14, winding the yarn 3 times round the needle for each stitch, K6, repeat from *, end K1.

Row 11:   yo, K2tog, K1, *(yo, K2tog) twice, yo, slip the next 14 stitches on to the right hand needle, dropping the extra loops, slip these 14 stitches back on to the left hand needle, purl 15 stitches together, (yo, K2tog) twice, yo, K2, repeat from *, end K1.

Row 12:   yo, K2tog, *K1, [(K1, P1 into yo), K1] 6 times, K1, repeat from *, end K2.

Repeat till you have knitted these twelve rows 15 times. Put stitches on a stitch holder, or a spare needle.

Knit a second half to match the first.

Graft the two halves together. Finish following instructions on page 15.

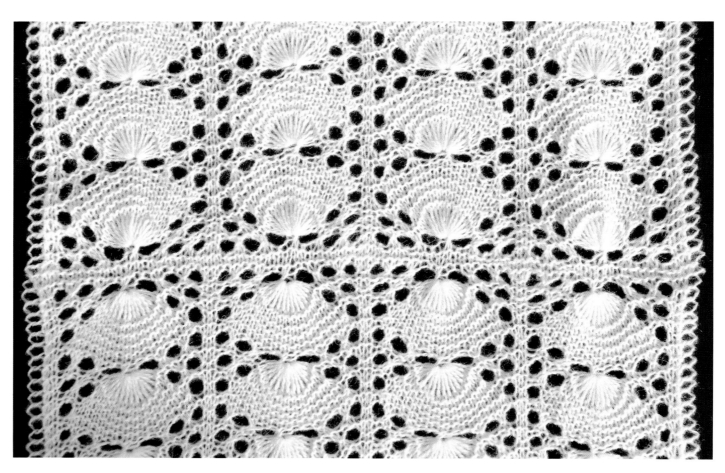

In Shetland dialect

Loosely lay on 80 loops, usin size 2.5 mm wires

Raas 1, 2, 5, 6, 9: cast, twa tagidder, mak ta da end.

Raa 3: cast, twa tagidder, 1, *cast, twa tagidder, 13, twa tagidder, cast, 2, repeat fae *, 1.

Raa 4: cast, twa tagidder, 1, *(mak an purl inta da cast), 15, *(mak an purl inta da cast), 2, repeat fae *, 1. (21 loops each repeat)

Raa 7: cast, twa tagidder, 1 *(cast, twa tagidder) twice, 11, (twa tagidder, cast) twice, 2, repeat fae *, 1.

Raa 8: cast, twa tagidder, 1 * (mak an purl inta da cast), 1, (mak an purl inta da cast), 13, (mak an purl inta da cast), 1, (mak an purl inta da cast), 2, repeat fae *, 1. (25 loops each repeat)

Raa 10: cast, twa tagidder, 1, *5, wind da yarn tree times roond da needle for da nixt 14 loops, 6, repeat fae *, 1.

Raa 11: cast, twa tagidder, 1, *(cast, twa tagidder) twice, cast, slip da nixt 14 loops on ta da right haand wire, drappin da extry loops, slip dis 14 loops back on to da left haand wire, purl 15 loops tagidder, (cast, twa tagidder) twice, cast, 2, repeat fae *, 1.

Raa 12: cast, twa tagidder, *1, [(mak an purl inta da cast), 1] 6 times, 1, repeat fae *, 2.

Repeat till you're med dis twal geng 15 times. Pit loops on a loop hadder, or a spare wire.

Mak a second half ta match da first.

Graft da twa haaves tagidder.

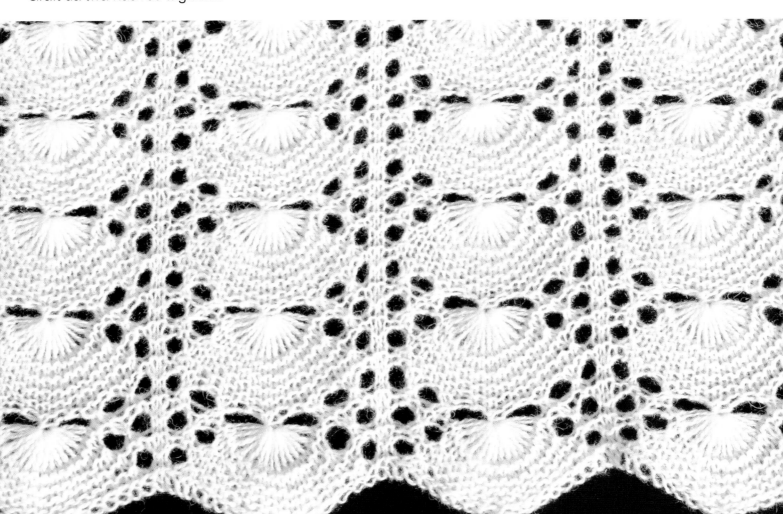

Chapelside Stole

Designed by Susan Johnson. Susan drafted this out as a challenge to herself. She was a student at Kathleen Anderson's lace knitting evening class and had come across a leaflet her mother had kept. In the 1960s, she had been as member of "The Knitters' Circle" run by Paton and Baldwins, now part of Coats Crafts. On the front of the leaflet was a picture of a stole knitted by Shetland lace knitter, Julia Sutherland, from yarn she had found in her stash. This yarn had been produced by Paton and Baldwins and discontinued by about 1902! There were no knitting instructions on the leaflet, so this pattern is an adaptation from the picture of the stole knitted fifty years ago.

Materials:

6 x 25g balls Shetland 1ply yarn

2 x 2.25 mm (UK 13, USA 0) knitting needles

Stitch holder or spare knitting needle

1 long, fine circular needle

Tapestry needle for grafting

Sizing:
Length 183 m (172 in.), width 48 cm (19in.)

Tension:
42 stitches, 30 rows for 10 cm (4in.)

Pattern Notes:
This stole is knitted in garter stitch throughout, in two parts which are then grafted together. The lace edging of the stole is then knitted on, following the instructions given. This uses an alternative method of attaching a lace edging to that used in the Voxter Scarf.

Take care in row 35 where you make an extra stitch in each motif by missing out one decrease per motif – this is to centre the motif. This makes the total number of stitches 179 for most of this motif. The 4 extra stitches are decreased in row 49 to complete the centering of this motif.

Instructions:
Cast on 175 stitches. Knit 10 rows.

Read all charts odd number rows from right, even number from left.

Work chart A from row 1 to row 122, working stitches 25 to 66 four times in each row.

Work chart B rows 1 to 90. Knit 2 rows.
Lay this piece of work aside retaining stitches on spare needle or stitch holder.
Work a second piece to match the first.
Continue on this second piece. Work chart C rows 1 to 53 seven times. Work stitches 10 to 21 thirteen times in each row. Then repeat rows 1 to 30 of chart C to finish.
Retain stitches on the needle; now garter stitch graft the two pieces according to the instructions on page 12.

Susan Johnson

Susan was four when she learned to knit, taught initially by her mother. She also received instruction at school from her class teachers and the visiting specialist knitting instructor.

She can remember receiving a favourite present for her seventh birthday of a knitting set comprising short knitting needles and rainbow coloured wool which she knit and re knit until it disintegrated!

While still in primary school and aged about ten she made skirts and Fair Isle cardigans for eight inch dolls and knitted miniature mittens which were attached to a gold safety pin and sold as brooches. These items were popular with tourists. While at secondary school (from age twelve) she made and sold Fair Isle berets, jumpers and cardigans.

Later she bought a knitting machine and knitted hand frame garments for sale. Even with all her industry, knitting has only ever provided a very small added income for Susan.

Susan has won prizes at Shetland Agricultural Shows and the Guild and has displayed at the Dornoch Fibrefest.

She hopes this book reaches everyone interested in Shetland, Shetland lace and knitting and that they receive and appreciate the spirit of quiet enjoyment that produced it.

Finish items before Christmas or it will 'craa at Christmas'.

Chapelside Stole chart A

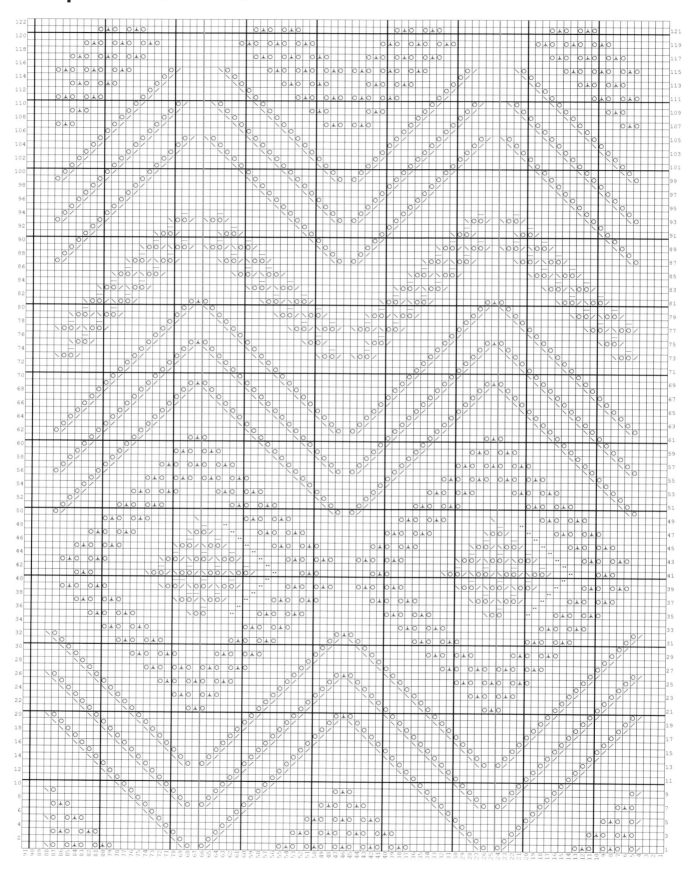

Chapelside Stole chart B

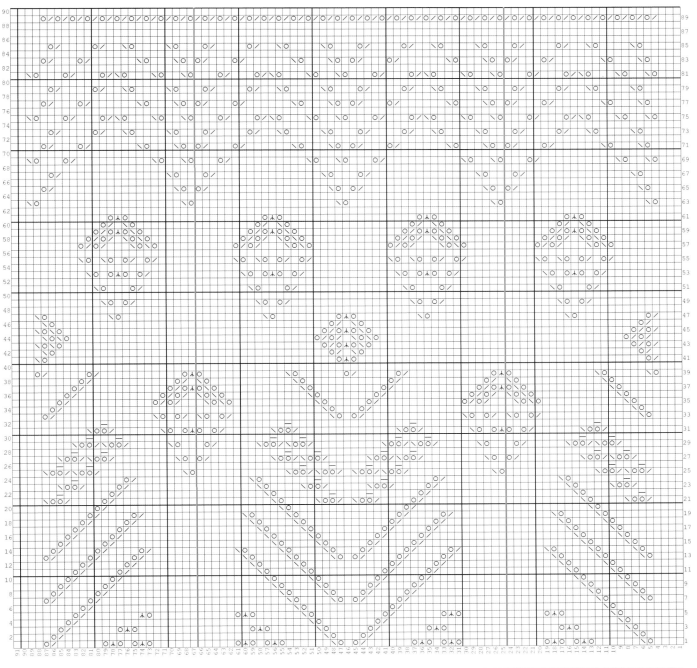

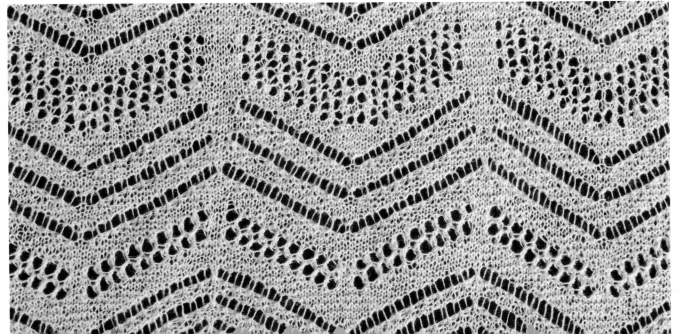

Edging:

Start at the corner of a short edge, *pick up the first 9 stitches, then every alternate stitch 78 times, then last 9 stitches (96 stitches for short edge). Pick up a stitch from the corner. Continue on the long edge, pick up every long loop, plus a stitch from the corner (432 stitches for long edge)*. Repeat from * to *. 1056 stitches.

To work edging: Cast on 12 stitches in waste yarn and knit a few rows. Change to main yarn and proceed according to Chart D at row 1. At end of row 2 and all even numbered rows, knit into back of last stitch on edging together with one stitch off circular needle.

This knitting on method of working the edging will finish with 24 scallops on each short edge and 108 scallops on each long edge.

When edging is complete, remove waste yarn and neatly graft the two edges together.

Wash and dress the completed stole according to the instructions on page 15.

Chapelside Stole chart C

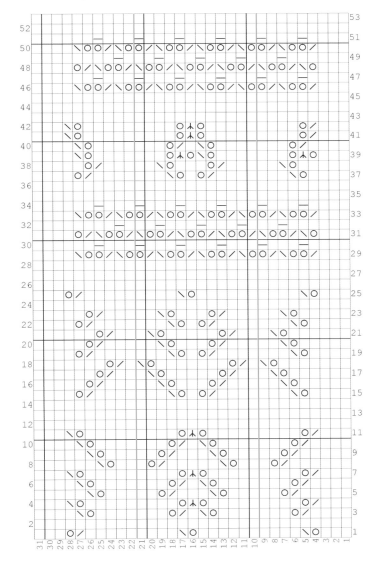

Chapelside Stole chart D

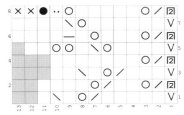

Sweerie bid sweerie an sweerie sat still. (Lazy person asks another lazy person to do something so nothing got done.)

Traditional Shetland Hap

Colour Designed and knitted by Zena Thomson. This Shetland hap is knitted in the traditional way.

Materials:
Jamieson & Smith 2 ply Shetland Jumper weight wool:

8 x 25 g balls: 27 (mid grey)

2 x 25 g: 1A (white), 5 (Shetland black), 78 (dark fawn)

1 x 25 g: 4 (moorit), 2 (fawn), 54 (dark grey), 203 (light grey)

OR, if you want to knit this in one shade only, 16 x 25g.

2 x 5 mm (UK 6, USA 8) knitting needles

Tapestry needle for grafting

Optional - markers to indicate corners of border, and/or border pattern repeats.

Sizing:
Width 122 cm (48 in.) depth 122cm (48in.)

Tension:
20 stitches, 36 rows for 10 cm (4 in.)

Pattern Notes:

This square hap is knitted in garter stitch throughout, starting with the narrow lace edging.

The lace edge is knitted as one piece; once all the other knitting has been done it's grafted together to form a square.

You may find it helpful to place a marker at end of every 16th scallop to indicate the corners.

Lace can be folded and secured with elastic/safety pin/thread to keep it under control as you knit.

The colourful borders, knitted in four quarters, are started from stitches picked from the straight edge of the lace. The border pattern is the Old Shell. After the middle has been knitted, the four quarters of the border are sewn together using the matching shades of wool. You can knit the borders of the hap in the round on a circular needle but will need to purl alternate rows. Knitting in the round saves sewing, and you can weave in ends as you knit.

The first four rows of the middle are knitted over stitches from all four quarters. The remainder of the middle is knitted from one quarter of the border, then grafted to the opposite quarter. As the middle is knitted, the last stitch of every row is knitted together with one stitch from the adjacent border, closing the square as you knit.

When changing colours, leave threads long enough to use when joining to adjacent quarter.

Instructions:

Da Lace

Using waste yarn, cast on 7 stitches and knit 2 or 3 rows. Join main colour (27) to knit lace edging, following chart A. Repeat chart A until you have 64 scallops. Slip these stitches on to a cotton thread (later they will be grafted to the start edge of the lace).

Traditional Shetland Hap chart A

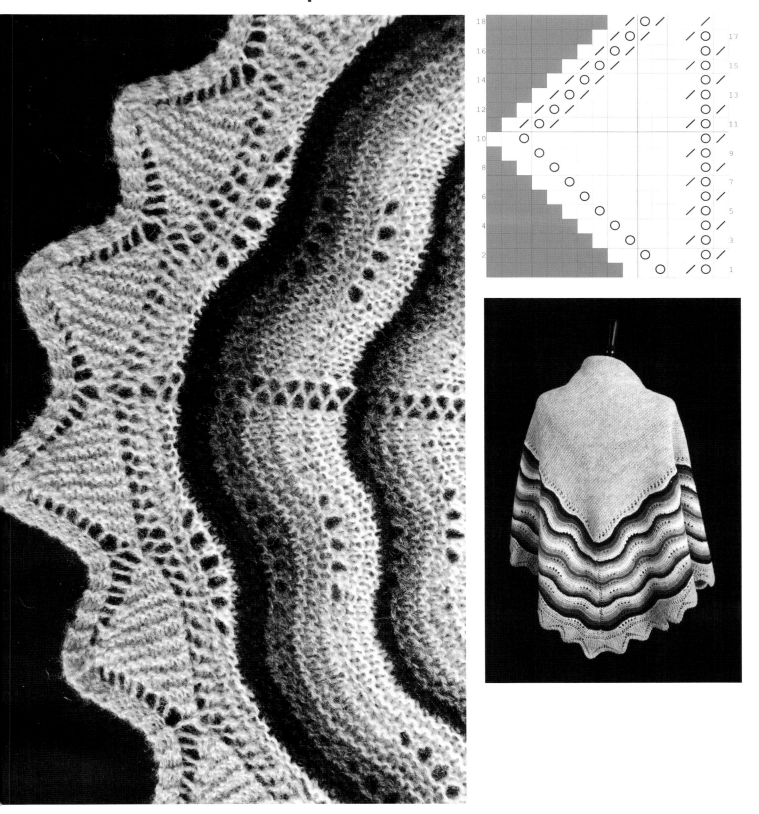

Da Boarder

To knit one quarter:

Pick up 144 stitches along the straight edge of the lace (16 scallops).

Secure the remaining lace with elastic/safety pin/thread.

Using main colour (27), knit one row.

Knit next row (colour 27): K1, yo, K2tog, K15, K2tog (K34, K2tog) 3 times, K16. (140 stitches) Break yarn.

Join white (1A) wool, leaving enough tail to sew to the adjacent quarter.

Follow chart B, working stitches 25-42 five times before knitting stitches 43-68.

Continue to work Chart B, remembering to change colours.

The colour sequence is:

2 rows 1A (white)

4 rows 5 (Shetland black)

4 rows 4 (moorit)

4 rows 78 (dark fawn)

2 rows 2 (fawn)

4 rows 1A (white)

2 rows 5 (Shetland black)

2 rows 54 (dark grey)

2 rows 27 (mid grey)

4 rows 203 (light grey)

4 rows 1A (white)

2 rows 2 (fawn)

4 rows 78 (dark fawn)

2 rows 4 (moorit)

note: colour sequence reverses after this row

4 rows 78 (dark fawn)

2 rows 2 (fawn)

4 rows 1A (white)

4 rows 203 (light grey)

2 rows 27 (mid grey)

2 rows 54 (dark grey)

2 rows 5 (Shetland black)

4 rows 1A (white)

2 rows 2 (fawn)

4 rows 78 (dark fawn)

4 rows 4 (moorit)

4 rows 5 (Shetland black)

2 rows 1A (white)

Complete Chart B, decreasing where indicated. (104 stitches)

Break yarn and put these stitches on a stitch holder or spare needle.

Repeat till you have three more quarters, matching the first.

Black yarn was supposed to be warmer than white so was used to make a vest for a delicate child. Grey was the softest and for knitting men's long drawers.

Chart (rows 1–82):

Row	Colour
81	1a White
77	5 Shetland Black
73	4 Moorit
69	78 Dark Fawn
67	2 Fawn
63	1a White
61	5 Shetland Black
59	54 Dark Grey
57	27 Mid Grey
53	203 Light Grey
49	1a White
47	2 Fawn
43	78 Dark Fawn
41	4 Moorit
37	78 Dark Fawn
35	2 Fawn
31	1a White
27	203 Light Grey
25	27 Mid Grey
23	54 Dark Grey
21	5 Shetland Black
17	1a White
15	2 Light Fawn
11	78 Dark Fawn
7	4 Moorit
3	5 Shetland Black
1	1a White

Traditional Shetland Hap chart B

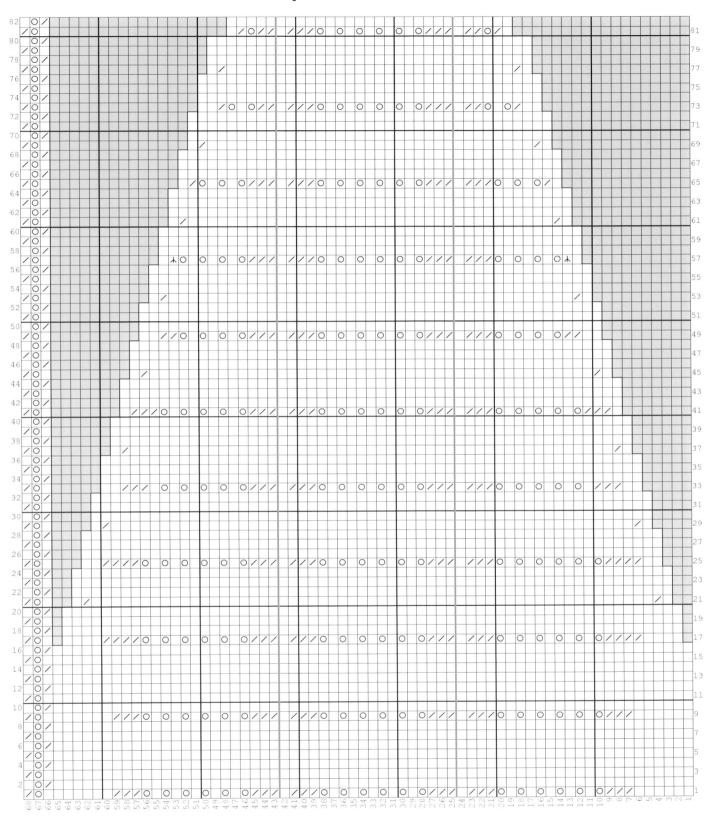

Middle

Gather stitches from all quarters on to one needle, right sides facing.

Join main colour (27).

Row 1: *K2, K2tog (K10, K2tog) 8 times, K2, yo, K2tog repeat from * (380 stitches – 95 for each quarter).

Rows 2 and 3: *K1 (yo, K2tog) 47 times* (this will take you to the end of the first quarter), repeat from * to * for each quarter.

Row 4: Knit. Break yarn.

Slip stitches from No 4 quarter on to a thread. Slip stitches from No1 quarter on to right hand knitting needle. Join yarn. Work on the stitches on No 2 quarter (this is for the middle).

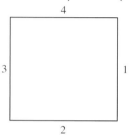

Row 1: K94, slip the next stitch, from No 3 quarter K2tog then pass the slipped stitch over. Turn

Row 2: K94, slip the next stitch, from No 1 quarter K2tog then pass the slipped stitch over. Turn

Row 3: K94, slip the next stitch, from No 3 quarter K1 then pass the slipped stitch over. Turn

Row 4: K94, slip the next stitch, from No 1 quarter K1 then pass the slipped stitch over. Turn

Repeat rows 3 and 4 until all stitches from No 1 and No 3 quarters have been used.

Graft the remaining stitches to No 4 quarter stitches.

At the beginning of lace scallops, unpick the waste yarn stitches till you have 7 stitches in main colour. Pick up 7 stitches of the last scallop. Graft these together, following instruction on page 12.

Sew corner seams, matching to colours used in the knitting.

Weave in ends.

Dress.

Changing the frequency, and sequence, of colour changes, as well as changing the number of rows between holes gives a completely different effect.

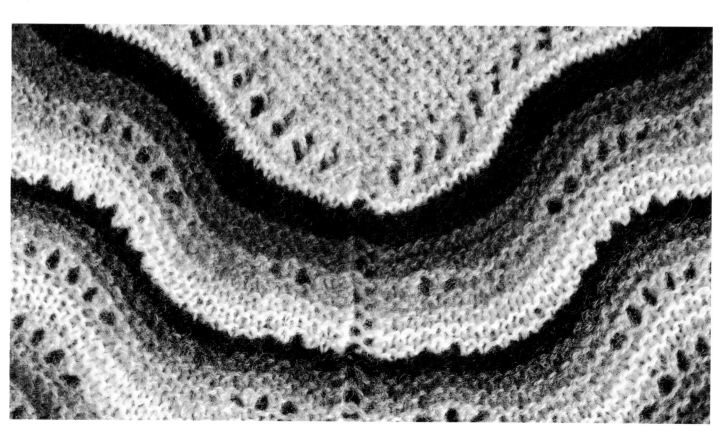

Glintin Gravit

Designed and knitted by Helen Robertson. The reflective yarn in this scarf glints in the light. This design is made from a lace edging pattern which has been mirrored to create this shape. This edging was chosen as it was the one knitted by her grandmother for the hap for Helen when she was a baby.

Materials:
1 X 25 g ball Shetland Organic yarn, single ply (or lace weight Shetland yarn)

1 x 10 g Retro-reflective yarn

2 X 7 mm (UK 2, USA 10.5) knitting needles

Sizing:
Approximate: Length 96 cm (38 in.) Width 24 cm (9.5 in.) at the widest part.

Tension:
28 stitches, 40 rows for 10 cm (4 in.)

Pattern Notes:
This scarf is knitted in garter stitch throughout.

The scarf has been designed so that it can be knitted right through and therefore no grafting is required.

Instructions:
Cast on 4 stitches, using one strand of each yarn. Increase 1 stitch at each end of every row by knitting twice into the first stitch and second last stitch till there are 8 stitches.
Next row: K3, yo, K2, yo, K3. (10 stitches)
Follow chart reading odd rows from the right and even rows from the left.
Knit rows 1 to 32. Knit rows 14 to 32, repeating as many times as you wish – this scarf has a total of 5 repeats. Work from row 14 to the end.
Cast off 4 stitches. Follow finishing instructions on page 15.

Helen Robertson

Helen learned to knit before she went to school. She had weekly knitting instruction during her time at primary school and had made a Lopi jumper by age eleven.

She continued to knit (and swear) through her teens and her first item for sale was a Fair Isle mouse made using a pattern from her knitting teacher. These sold in the Shetland Museum and were very popular.

Helen now enjoys designing and knitting using wire and makes jewellery using silver and enamelled copper wire.

She was commissioned to knit wire Shetland lace lampshades for the Shetland Museum and Archives. She recently completed a project entitled 'Hentilagaets' which aimed to put Shetland lace patterns back into the landscape that generated them by knitting lace wire sections into an agricultural fence and in the window and wall of a derelict croft house. She currently sells knitted jewellery in the Shetland Museum shop, local galleries and online through her website (www. helenrobertson.co.uk) and Facebook page www.facebook.com/helenrobertsonjewellery.

She has contributed to a book entitled 'Jewellery Using Textile Techniques' and runs an evening class entitled 'Knit Your Own Jewellery'.

She hopes this book will entice folk to try a bit of Shetland lace and will provide a snapshot of Shetland knitters and their lives.

Glintin Gravit

This is part of Laura Friedlander's poem,

'Knitting Tradition'

With the belt round her waist
 she sat by the fire
 with the fine lace shawl
 laid up on the wires.
 In her heart she would quietly sing
 as she knitted the shawl
 to slip through her own wedding ring.
 The stitches, the patterns,
 the tales that they gave
 and in these patterns
 her history was saved
 bird's eye, cat's paw, print an da wave .

The following year her son so small
 wrapped up in tradition
 and the fine lace shawl.

Laura Friedlander 2012

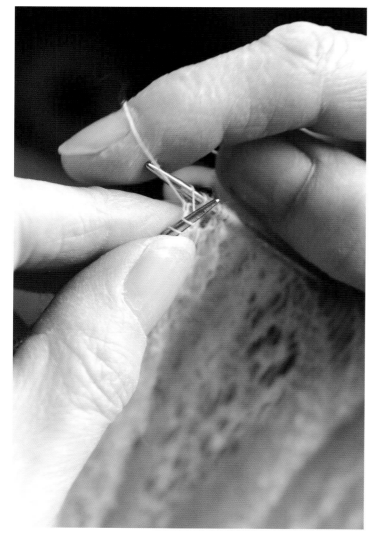

Laura Friedlander

Laura Friedlander's two great passions of literature and textiles were established during her childhood and are given free rein in her life today as she continues to work on her own writing projects whilst researching and studying the history of knitwear in particular.

Laura says: "At school in Sandwick during the 1970s my favourite lesson was the knitting lesson on a Friday morning. It was the highlight of my week, and started me off on my love of knitting."

"My maternal grandmother was a fantastic knitter and I was determined to learn her skills too and carry on the tradition in another generation."

"Other knitting techniques were learned when my mother was a home help to a lady in Hoswick. I was only eleven at the time and a small skinny child. I think the elderly lady my mother cared for took pity on me! She sat me on a creepie and showed me how to knit rib for gloves and I still use the same methods that she showed me even now. I never leave home without two items, my note/sketchbook and a little knitting bag which usually contains a pair of socks in progress!"

Joyce Ward

Joyce cannot remember learning to knit, but her first memory is of knitting mittens and puzzling over how one thumb was smaller than the other. This was probably when she was aged about eleven. Getting knitting lessons at school were a highlight of her week.

Joyce sold her first knitted item when in her twenties, when she concentrated on machine knitted fisherman's rib jumpers. Machine knitting, then a spell working for Jamieson & Smith, used to provide Joyce with her main income, and gave her the opportunity to attend Woolfest and Knitting and Stitching shows to demonstrate and teach.

She has always knitted for family and friends, and always has socks 'on da wires' for knitting in the car. She has phases of knitting lace and Fair Isle. Over the years she has learned a great deal from people paid to teach knitting.

Becoming the fastest knitter at a Knitting and Stitching Show in Harrogate earned Joyce a prize of £100. She used this to buy a spinning wheel, and learned to spin.

To pass on her skills, Joyce bullies as many of her friends, family and acquaintances as possible to try knitting or spinning. She meets a group of friends once a month for a 'Knit Day' – she often 'sprets' (takes back) for other folk and gets them going again. Joyce has also passed on her sock knitting skills by instructing at evening classes.

Joyce's task in the preparation of this book has been to prepare all the charts using DesignaKnit software (www.softbyte.co.uk) and write the instructions for several of the patterns. This came ahead of her own intention to submit a pattern for the book. Her diligence, ability to read and understand written and charted patterns, and her attention to detail is greatly appreciated by all contributors.

Joyce is pleased to have been part of this collaboration and has learnt a great deal in the process. She hopes it will encourage local knitters to join the Guild, or at least try lace knitting. She also believes a book about Shetland knitting, written by Shetlanders, is long overdue.

Acknowledgements

The seeds of the idea to produce this book were sown in the early years of this century in a conversation between Winnie Balfour and Mary Kay. Both are members of Shetland Guild of Spinners, Knitters, Weavers and Dyers.

Once Winnie and Mary decided to foster the idea they enlisted the help of other Guild members, Ina Irvine, Zena Thomson and Hazel Tindall who have experience of designing and writing knitting patterns. Other members were asked if they too would submit patterns for the book.

Joyce Ward, whose experience of writing knitting patterns and her expertise in producing all the graphs in the book became a key member of the group. Pearl Johnson and Susan Johnson provided designs, test knitted and assisted during the final stages of production.

Kathleen Anderson provided two complete patterns. Sue Arthur provided a written pattern and Lauretta Robertson gave two items for which patterns were written. All three helped with test knitting. Helen Robertson assembled biographies, often prising detail from over-modest contributors. Helen also provided the mannequin for the photographs. Various other Guild members, family and friends have helped by test knitting patterns from the written instructions and graphs, often without the help of any photograph to guide them – a real test!

We are grateful to Mary Sinclair and the family of the late Gilda Johnson for giving permission to reproduce one of her patterns.

Throughout all stages Winnie was the co-ordinator, making sure momentum was maintained, and frequently driving many miles each week to discuss and check minute detail in graphs and written instructions. Electronic communication has been beneficial too for checking written instructions and graphs, sharing ideas, making decisions as well as reducing the chance for errors to creep in between designer and publisher.

Designing and knitting is something all the contributors do, using knowledge and practices passed down generations. Providing detailed written instructions for knitters of all levels to replicate their design is less usual, and often more time-consuming, than the original knitting. Some designed, knitted and wrote the patterns; others wrote the instructions for items designed and knitted by colleagues. All donated their designs freely to Shetland Guild of Spinners, Knitters, Weavers and Dyers.

Too often a beautiful piece of knitting can be spoiled by poor finishing so we have made every effort to include detailed instructions to ensure pleasing results. We are indebted to Kathleen Anderson who did the grafting and knitting for the photographs.

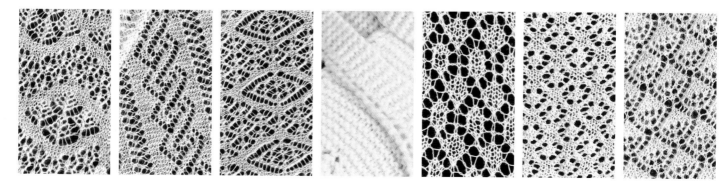

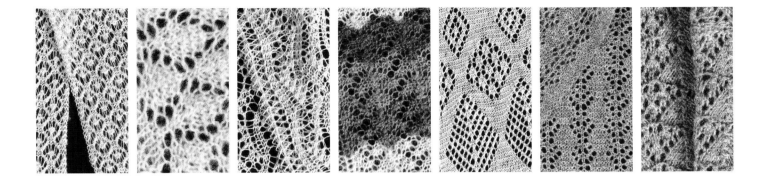

Over several years Joyce James from Canada has led groups of knitting, weaving and spinning enthusiasts to visit Shetland. On each visit she arranges time for them to meet with Shetland Guild members. In 2011 one of her group anonymously donated a large sum of money to the Guild, specifiying that Bess Jamieson should decide how it should be used to benefit the Guild. Bess suggested it be used to help with production costs of this book, in particular the photography. Photographing fine lace is never easy so we are indebted to Dave Donaldson for the fine job he has done. We are grateful to Bolts (Shetland) Ltd for providing space suitable for photography.

The sheep are from Jennie and Andy Bradley's flock of pure bred Shetland sheep. They produce high quality, prize-winning fleeces which are highly sought after, especially by hand spinners.

Sharon Miller's book *Heirloom Knitting* has been a valuable modern resource. If our book has inspired you to design your own lace projects, you too should find Sharon's book very useful.

Staff at The Shetland Times Ltd., especially Charlotte Black, have been encouraging throughout. Designers Andrew Morrison and Melvyn Leask's skills enhanced and helped achieve this attractive and useful book.

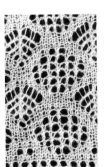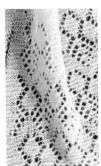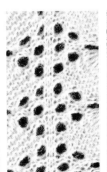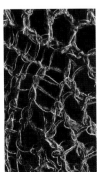